When the Waves Came

When the Waves Came

MW Larson

CHIN MUSIC PRESS

spring 2020

Library of Congress Cataloging in Publication data is available.

ISBN: 978-1-63405-981-7

Published by Chin Music Press
1501 Pike Place #329
Seattle, WA 98101-1542
www.chinmusicpress.com

First [1] edition

Paperback original

For Junko, and for all the people of Tohoku

今荒城の夜半の月　変はらぬ光誰がためぞ

垣に残るはただ葛松に歌ふはただ嵐

天上影は変はらねど　栄枯は移る世の姿

映さんとてか今も尚　ああ荒城の夜半の月

土井晩翠

Now, over the ruined castle the midnight moon,

Its light unchanged; for whom does it shine?

In the hedge, only the laurel is left behind:

In the pines, only the wind of the storm still sings.

High in the heavens the light remains unchanged.

Glory and decay are the mark of this shifting earth.

Is it to copy them now, brighter yet,

Over the ruined castle the midnight moon

—Bansui Doi

Translated by Geoffrey Bowas and Anthony Thwaite

Table of Contents

Prologue

Tremors

Columbus, Ohio

I remember when the quake struck, or rather, the moment after, when the woman I was in love with called. It was Friday morning, just before 1:00 a.m., and I was in my cramped apartment at my desk, which was lit by the pale-blue glow of my laptop and covered in stacks of my students' essays. The college writing class I'd been teaching during the winter term was over, and the only thing between me and spring break was nineteen final papers. In Japan, it would be past noon, and Junko would be working at International Travel, an agency owned by her aunt in Mutsu, a small city in Aomori Prefecture. Every day, we talked during her lunch break, but her call was two hours late.

"Hey," I said, picking up my cell phone. She usually called on Skype, so I asked, "You want me to login? I can turn on my video."

"There was an earthquake. A big one," she said. "It must've shook for two minutes."

"Are you okay?"

"There's no damage. For a second I thought the ceiling was going to cave in."

This didn't seem unusual; actually, in a way, I was jealous. I'd been an English teacher in her hometown for two years, and one day while at work at Odaira Middle School a rumbling had risen from the ground, and the walls of the teacher's office began to tremble as the whine of tsunami sirens echoed out of the port. I sat frozen at my desk, waiting for the order to evacuate, though the Japanese teachers turned back to their computers the moment the shaking stopped. It had been a small quake, and the school soon resumed its regular rhythm. By the time I left Japan, I'd begun to enjoy these tremors, especially when they came at night: the sense of my consciousness floating up through the murky waters of sleep, breaching the surface of the black ocean for an instant, and then, after glimpsing the shadows on the ceiling, sinking back down to the depths where my dreams were waiting. After I moved back to the States for graduate school, earthquakes were just part of what I missed about Mutsu.

"Mom called and said the tsunami sirens are sounding," Junko's voice was dull with shock, but she didn't seem afraid. "She's going to the elementary school with Dad, just to be safe."

"I'm sure it'll be fine," I said.

"Yeah, right." She exhaled. I pictured her in a wheeled office chair, her cell phone pressed to her ear.

"What are you going to do with the power out?"

"Maybe I'll get lucky and we'll close early."

I laughed and, to help her forget about the quake, started to complain about my grading: how many of my kids had fallen back on the writing habits they'd entered my class with, how so few of them had taken to heart my advice that the English language is not a blunt instrument.

I knew Junko was worried about her father getting to the evacuation area. Half a year earlier they'd learned he had cancer, but by the time the doctors discovered the malignant cells, those cells had already spread from his lungs to his bones. He was stage four, on chemo, and doing his best to fight it. A few days before, she'd told me he was having trouble eating and had lost a lot of strength.

Junko had learned of her dad's condition after I'd left, at a time when, with the Pacific Ocean between us, our relationship was unsteady.

We'd first met at a wine-tasting event, and I was immediately taken by her smile and cynical sense of humor. I'd come to Mutsu after finishing college, my head full of memories of my former homestay family's warmth and images of the city on the outskirts of Tokyo where I'd studied abroad. I'd figured I could teach for a year and plan my next step in life. But instead of one of the country's metropolises, I was assigned to a small city on the northern tip of the main island. I spent most of my first year adapting to the cold and sense of isolation. By my second year, I'd begun to feel at home in the city. When Junko told me she worked for a travel agency, I recognized the company.

A few days after the wine tasting, I went to International Travel to book a Shinkansen ticket to Tokyo; I could've made the bullet train reservation online, but I was curious about her. After she'd typed the details of my trip into her computer and printed out my tickets, I leaned across the counter and, under my breath, asked if she'd be free for dinner someday. On our first date, we went to the city's only French restaurant and then to a bar, where we drank until we felt brave enough to kiss.

Over the course of more evenings spent in more bars and restaurants, we stumbled into a relationship. Things between us felt right and soon it was natural for her to drop by my apartment on the weekends or invite me to grab a drink with her work friends. The only hitch was that I'd enrolled in a graduate writing program back in the States. I planned to keep teaching in Mutsu until the spring, fly back to the US over the summer, and then find an apartment in central Ohio before courses started in the fall. I'd told Junko I was planning on going back when we met, but, back then, this fact had been but a distant cloud on the horizon. By the time I was boarding the train to the airport, the skies had darkened, and fate was about to start pouring down on us.

I'd failed at long-distance dating enough times to know better than to try again, so we kept things ambiguous: no promises as to what would happen once we were on different continents. But we stayed in touch, and, late that fall—not long after her family got the results of her dad's CT scan—she came to Columbus and confided that her father was in a bad way. What I felt for her wasn't pity, but respect for the honesty with which she faced the situation. In spite of everything, we were still together and had been making things work for nine months on March 11, 2011.

We only stayed on the phone for a few minutes after the earthquake. With the power out, Junko couldn't charge her cell phone, and she needed to save her battery for an emergency, so we said goodbye. I didn't know it then, but it would be the last I'd hear from her for a long time.

Those were the last moments before the phone networks across Tohoku were jammed with calls as people realized the extent of the disaster. Seismic sensors had triggered shutdowns at eleven nuclear reactors, and, within minutes, twenty percent of the country's atomic energy was offline. In a country where a third of all electricity came from nuclear power, this meant a huge shortfall of wattage: in blackouts that would stretch on for days, over four million people would lose power. Junko was one of them.

After hanging up with her I slept for a few hours. But, before long, I began to toss and turn, half-conscious of my cellphone buzzing with texts from my family and friends asking if the people I knew—Junko, my former colleagues in Mutsu, my old homestay family, who lived less than a mile from the coast in Chiba Prefecture—were safe. As I woke up and read their messages my first sleepy thought was, safe from what? Even after I got up and checked the *New York Times'* website, where the headline read "Huge Quake Triggers Tsunami Off Japan's Coast," next to a picture of a wave of mud crushing a home, I thought it was an overreaction, typical of the American news media.

Earthquakes large enough to get national news coverage in other countries are reported in passing before the local weather in Japan. The islands that make up the country are dotted with a series of active volcanoes that periodically smoke, shake, and erupt, and, lying off the northeastern coast of Asia, the archipelago is in a corridor traveled by ten or twenty typhoons a year. The country's close relationship with disaster is acknowledged in the English language—the word tsunami is taken from the Japanese word for harbor wave—as well as in the American popular imagination, where scenes of refugees fleeing cityscapes flattened by Godzilla have long influenced our ideas of catastrophe.

Floods, landslides, and gale-force winds are facts of life there. When I was teaching in Mutsu, much like the locals, I'd come to hold a shrugging attitude toward the tremors that shook the small city and the rain that regularly turned the road next to my apartment into a rushing torrent. They were rarely used, but I knew there were safety measures to counter every danger: evacuation areas for each district in the towns and villages, tsunami barriers and breakers surrounding every coastal city. Any waves generated by the earthquake would surely crash ineffectually against these concrete walls.

So, on Friday morning, as usual, I slowly made myself a bowl of oatmeal. Knowing cable news wouldn't miss an earthquake of that magnitude, I turned on my TV and flipped to CNN, only to find how wrong I'd been.

Above the familiar news ticker, water was washing away a village. The camera zoomed in and I made out several cars in the flow—the feed switched, and, in the next video, a current swept up a channel, crushing a boat against a bridge. For a moment I thought maybe the network was replaying footage from a different disaster—the 2004 Indonesian Tsunami, perhaps—but then I heard Anderson Cooper's steady voice narrating the tape. The things he was saying were so terrible they seemed to have been pulled from the script of a Hollywood disaster film.

Near Tokyo, fires from an oil refinery sent pillars of black smoke into the sky. Photos showed the Sendai airport terminal looking like an island in a floodplain. These images played in a loop and among them was a video of a single white fishing boat caught in a whirlpool off the shore of a town called Oarai. I could see the flooded village in the background as the vessel spun around the maelstrom, and, while it circled, I lapsed into an open-mouth trance. The shock was like a drug: I could understand the effects but had no power to resist them. I'd later learn that the vortex was the result of the ocean's water rushing to fill a crack in the crust of the earth, as if the Pacific was a giant bathtub and the quake had dislodged the plug; the boat was like a toy sucked into the swirl above the drain.

I ran back to my bedroom, where my laptop was. I started calling Junko on Skype, clicking the green dial icon over and over. Each time there was a pause, and, after one ring, a click before a recording came on and a woman's voice said she couldn't connect me to the number I'd dialed. Of course, she couldn't.

Unable to reach anyone, I sat in front of the television and gave myself over to images of disaster. Waves strewn with boards rushed through the streets of a city, lifting tile-roofed buildings from their foundations; waves cascaded over the cement walls of an inland channel, the water quickly turning into a flow of muddy debris; whole, intact houses on fire and floating on the waves; waves moving like living things as they churned across the land. Then, once the surges had stilled, came the images of flooded towns, houses sunk up to their roofs, cars bobbing bedside boats, and unchecked fires burning through the buildings that stood above the water.

Watching the footage filled me with a mixture of shock and dread, but I couldn't stop staring at the television. A friend of mine, who'd lived in Tokyo, told me she'd had a similar compulsion; for her, watching was the only way she had of acknowledging the pain she felt as she saw a place in which she'd lived—a place she cared about—being destroyed.

I'd moved around a lot over the previous seven years—from Rainier, Washington, my hometown, to New Hampshire, for college, and then to Washington D.C. and New York—and over that time my years in the Tohoku region had been the longest I'd stayed in one place. While I was there, I'd learned how to hold down a job, what it meant to be a teacher, and how to adapt to a culture different from my own. Though I didn't realize it until I saw the devastation, it was still one of the places I thought of as home. A place I felt an obligation to.

I hadn't been able to reach Junko, but, after a few hours, I did manage to contact the daughter of my former homestay family. When I'd first gone to Japan as a college student, I'd been placed with the Gokitas in the prefecture east of Tokyo, only two kilometers from the coast—but Akemi told me they were safe. They lived well south of the epicenter and hadn't seen any waves, though they'd heard houses and businesses on the shore had been damaged.

Soon, my friends up north on the Shimokita Peninsula, the axe-shaped cape at the top of Honshu where Mutsu was, began posting on Facebook saying they were okay. It was reassuring to know the entire city hadn't been hit, but my friends all lived in the interior of the peninsula while Junko's home was in Ohata, which had been a fishing town before it was incorporated into Mutsu. It was only a couple minutes walk from her house to the port, and I knew even a medium-sized wave would decimate her neighborhood. The city was two hundred miles from the rupture that had caused the quake, but it was also on the coast. What scared me the most were the images coming out of Hachinohe City: huge cargo ships being picked up by the waves and thrown onto the concrete docks. It was only a two-hour drive from there to Mutsu.

I did my best to finalize the grades for my class, but, as I tried to read my student's papers, my mind kept drifting back to the tsunami, and I found myself staring blankly at the wall beside my desk, thinking about what could be happening over there.

Then, on the morning of March 12, after thirty hours, I finally got a text from Junko. Her cell didn't have much battery, she wrote that she was messaging me one last time before it died: *Last night we didn't have heat, so I laid in bed with all my clothes on, too scared to sleep. The phones are out. We don't know when the power will return. People are saying hundreds of bodies are washing up in Iwate and Sendai. We might lose water at any time. Waves keep coming, the tsunami warning sirens ring through the town, and no one is on the streets. It's like a zombie movie.* I knew that early in March it would be freezing; there would still be snow on the ground. *This town*, she wrote, *is like a place in hell.*

I messaged her back, telling her to look after her family—that they'd get through this—but she didn't respond. Even as the number of dead and missing kept climbing, I felt a selfish sense of relief knowing the tsunami hadn't reached her home.

After I heard from Junko, I was able to wrap up my class, and then my father called. My mother had texted that morning, but she and my dad had long been divorced and I'd wondered if he'd seen the news. He said MSNBC was reporting that the death toll was in the tens of thousands.

"No," I said, willing it not to be true. "It won't be so bad. They're prepared for this."

"There's also this reactor they're having problems with," he said. "Fukuishi or something?"

"I'm sure the Fukushima plant had a seawall. They'll have been ready."

I told him how each school I'd taught in had practiced evacuation drills, in which the teachers led their students to high ground. I explained how every coastal city and town I'd ever seen was surrounded by breakwaters and rings of tsunami defenses.

But of course, I was wrong. Executives at TEPCO, the Tokyo Electric Power Company, who had been operating the damaged power plant, had put off building a sufficiently high seawall, despite the warnings from geologists and regulators. The coastal towns near the epicenter were also unprepared for such a large quake, or for swells that in some places reached over 130 feet high. Though I didn't see it then, now I understand that evacuation drills and disaster training are plans for events that cannot be predicted; we practice crouching under desks and leading children out into fields but, as a species, we are woefully incapable of anticipating nature's destructive power.

The Great Tohoku Earthquake and Tsunami was a release of thousands of years of seismic energy, and, in economic terms, it would prove to be more expensive than any natural disaster before it. An undersea, megathrust quake, shifted parts of Honshu two meters closer to North America, stretching the land itself, and even affecting the length of the earth's days. My father had been right: in a few minutes, over ten-thousand lives had been lost, and, over the next several days, the toll would climb to over eighteen-thousand dead and missing.

When electricity was restored to Mutsu two days after the quake, Junko called me on Skype, and I was relieved to see her in the square of the video window, looking a little shaken. Her image was blurred by the poor connection and her black hair was mussed. She hadn't slept or showered. I was glad just to see her face.

"The gas stations are all closed," she said when I suggested she and her parents might be better off driving to one of their relatives' houses. "Besides, the highway is blocked to the south. Nothing's being delivered, all the shelves in the convenience stores are empty."

Despite these hardships, the worst, it seemed, had passed for Mutsu. However, in the disaster zone, search and rescue crews were just beginning to arrive as the Self-Defense Forces cleared the roads and helped survivors to evacuation centers. Off the coast of Sendai, the USS Ronald Regan was providing aerial relief to those trapped by the tsunami, and, inside the containment buildings of several reactors at the Fukushima Daiichi Nuclear Power Plant, a dangerous amount of pressurized hydrogen was building up. Members of the foreign and domestic media were rushing to Tohoku even as citizens streamed out of the region, and, back in Tokyo, Naoto Kan—the country's embattled prime minister—was scrambling to assess the damage caused by the tsunami and trying to get in touch with TEPCO.

In the following weeks, life outside the tsunami-afflicted areas settled into a new normal, and Junko and I resumed our nightly calls. TV news networks in the US soon turned their attention to a fresh conflict in Libya, occasionally taking a break from the NATO bombing campaign to report on the progress of the meltdowns at the Fukushima nuclear station or to tally up the growing number of dead from the tsunami as more bodies were pulled from the wreckage. I kept coming back to that video shot from a helicopter off the coast of Oarai of a fishing boat caught in the spinning flow. I would watch the vessel circling the foaming white center of the vortex on the little YouTube screen, unable to know if there was a person inside, until—right before the undertow sucked the craft below the surface—the footage cut out. I came to see this image as a metaphor for people outmatched by the forces surrounding them: currents that can be fully comprehended only from a distance at which it is impossible to help those swept up in the surge. The sense of being cut off and isolated was a feeling I grew intimate with as, from halfway around the world, I examined the ruins of a place I was still connected to—a place I felt I had to get back to.

At the time, I thought of my affinity for the country in terms of the years I'd spent there and the opportunities it had given me. When I'd graduated from college in 2008, the financial crisis had been looking worse every day, and I was grateful to be hired as a middle school English teacher through the Japanese Exchange and Teaching Program, to have a job and a chance to think about the next phase of my life while so many people were struggling just to find work. My salary had been paid by the citizens of Mutsu, a city similar to many of those ravaged by the tsunami.

Though the disaster hadn't touched me, I was still shaken, confused. Even though my master's program was in the US and my grandparents lived in Cleveland, just two and a half hours up the interstate from Columbus, I wondered whether I'd made the right choice in coming back to the States.

I'd been splitting my time between graduate coursework and teaching college writing to support myself, but I didn't have plans for the summer. I asked Junko to help me look into the possibility of volunteering with the post-tsunami cleanup, and she sent me a link to Caritas Kamaishi—a branch of Caritas Internationalis—a charity affiliated with the Vatican. I wasn't Catholic, but the organization welcomed volunteers of all faiths and had base camps in three coastal cities in Tohoku.

Those were the months when people up and down the Sanriku coast were picking through the wreckage of their cities and towns, while, to the south, the Fukushima Daiichi nuclear plant lurched from one catastrophe to another. It was the start of half a dozen years when, in the aftermath of the disaster, the sense of vulnerability that had infected Japanese society since the early 1990s bloomed into a full-blown crisis, and the country abandoned the internal reforms it had been undertaking, doubling down on the institutions and leaders that had served it in the past.

It was the summer I returned to volunteer with the recovery effort, and the year the chemo proved futile and the cancer spread through Junko's father's body. For her and me, it was also the beginning of a series of moves between Middle America and Tohoku, which brought us together and then forced us apart, as we tried to figure out what we meant to one another. It was a time when I found a life I never could have imagined and, in communities torn apart by the tsunami, discovered a country different from the one I'd thought I known.

Loss

March 2011

I. A Colossal Swell

Kamaishi City, Iwate Prefecture

Before the snow and the strangers huddled around a kerosene heater, before the screams, before the bodies in the half-flooded bus, before the ringing sirens and the roar of rushing water, before the shattered windows and broken appointments, before the floor started vibrating, Keitaro Matsumoto was smoking one of his thin Kent cigarettes at 2:45 p.m. on March 11, taking a break between customers.

His beauty salon, Hair Studio K, occupied a single room on the second floor of a building that was owned by a landlord from Chiba and also housed a fish monger's shop on the first floor. He'd rented the space in the city's Owatari district for twenty-five years, along with the apartment next to it, where he lived alone.

Saturday was usually his busiest day, but that week many of his customers had made Friday reservations. At 3:00 p.m., Mrs. Kikuchi was coming for her usual bob cut, and he'd scheduled several appointments after her. His legs were already stiff from standing, and his right hand was tired from squeezing the scissors. Cutting hair was tiring, but he enjoyed it and noticed his exhaustion only during the pauses in his day; he'd had many worse jobs and he knew he was lucky.

Keitaro had come to his profession in a roundabout way: upon finishing high school he'd moved to Sendai, the biggest city in the Tohoku region, to attend a one-year hospitality-training program. But, after working in an actual hotel for less than a year, he was let go and started hopping from one part-time job to another, living in tenements, and constantly on the verge of homelessness. He lost weight, dropping over forty pounds, until he felt weak, sickly, and broken by city life. Several months passed before he found regular work at the Queen Salon, sweeping up hair and checking in customers at the front desk. He learned the beautician's trade from the other employees, one task at a time, and within a year he'd earned his cosmetology license through a correspondence course.

Before long, he returned to his hometown to open his own shop. He'd worked hard to build his business, and, though there was still plenty he wanted to do, he'd made a decent sort of life for himself. Hair Studio K was small, but Keitaro had a good location and loyal customers.

His next client that day, Mrs. Kikuchi, had been coming to him since he'd first opened his doors. Like him, she was in her fifties, and the short cut she always asked for suggested she'd put away the better part of her vanity.

He was still waiting, considering another cigarette, when the floor started vibrating beneath his feet. The shaking moved up into the walls, the ceiling. Keitaro was used to earthquakes and the tremors didn't scare him. But the quake's sound kept expanding, and when it hadn't stopped after a minute—it seemed to be only getting stronger—he knew this was a big one. The floor was shaking so hard he couldn't walk.

Cans of hair spray rattled off a shelf and cracked against the linoleum. He cursed these nuisances with an everyday sense of annoyance.

His salon had a view of the city's main street, and the two-story buildings across from him were trembling as light poles swayed like saplings in a strong wind. A crack snaked up from the bottom corner of his window; he watched the fissure until it stopped sliding across the pane—in the next instant the glass shattered and fell in, scattering shards everywhere. With the floor lurching back and forth beneath his feet, a panic grew in him, erasing his irritation.

Then, just as the entire building seemed about to come crashing down, the vibrations weakened. The shaking subsided, and slowly his shop settled into its usual quiet. He took what felt like his first breath in a long time, as his heart hammered against his chest. A couple minutes later, the wails of tsunami warning sirens rose into the air.

When he'd lived in Sendai, Keitaro had been through the 1978 Miyagi Earthquake, which he thought had been almost as violent as that day's, and, since returning to his hometown, big quakes had shaken the region in 1994 and 2005. He'd seen his share of broken windows and fallen roof tiles, but a tsunami hadn't touched Kamaishi in decades. Over the past few months, something about the pattern of tremors had reminded him of the days before the quake in Sendai. He'd even told one of his customers he thought another big one was on the way, though, even if his prediction was right, Kamaishi had done a lot to prepare.

In 2009, after thirty-one years and over $1.5 billion, the city had finished construction on a massive system of breakwaters to protect the port and boost Kamaishi's dwindling steel industry. They'd held a ceremony in which the Guinness World Records people presented the mayor with a certificate recognizing the breakers as the deepest in the world.

Still, Keitaro was worried about his elderly mother, who lived with his older brother and his brother's wife in the house where he'd been raised. His brother and his brother's wife would both be at their jobs, and their workplaces were far enough inland to be safe, but his mother was alone, watching over the house in Ryoishi, a low-lying district of the city vulnerable to tsunamis. In 1960, a wave triggered by an earthquake off the coast of Chile had decimated the area, and, afterward, they'd built a seawall along the beach: a giant concrete barrier over twenty feet high.

Though his mother didn't get around very well anymore, her instinct would be to flee, and she might hurt herself in the process; she'd need help getting to the evacuation area up in the hills. He thought to call home, but, when he checked his phone, he saw he wasn't getting cell service, and then he noticed the entire salon had lost power. Part of him was beginning to understand the quake had been even bigger than he'd guessed.

Although he couldn't get a signal, he had a message from Mrs. Kikuchi, which she must've sent before the power went out: *With the earthquake, I just can't make it.* But he'd already assumed the rest of his appointments that day were canceled.

Keitaro decided to make the ten-minute drive to his familial home to check on his mother. First though, in case a tsunami did come, he began to pack up his tools—his scissors, shears, and combs. As long as he had these, he'd have his livelihood. He was gathering the last of his things when, out the broken window, he saw water pouring into the street.

It took only a few seconds for the road to disappear beneath the churning flow. He felt as if his feet were bolted to the floor, and he couldn't move as the waves covered the asphalt. At first, the water was like a clear gushing stream, but soon it turned a polluted gray. Fish flopped for their lives in the flow and a huge, round log floated by, but this didn't strike him as odd. He didn't think about his car parked out back, which would already be ruined, or how quickly everything in his world had changed; he didn't quite grasp what he'd lost. Instead, what struck him—watching the water rise toward the top of the first floor and knowing he was trapped—was how isolated he was.

Later, he'd see how the sudden terror of the tsunami had crystallized his regrets; chief among these was that he hadn't found anyone to share his life with. He'd been married once in his youth, but it had lasted only a few years before he and his wife had divorced. In the back of his mind, he still hoped he would find someone. But, in the moment, he didn't think of any of these things. He only knew he had to escape.

He left his tools on the counter, went out into the hall, and saw the water was rising in the stairwell—it was nearly to the top of the first floor. The waves had smashed in the door to the street and broken pieces of wood floated in the deluge. A sewer smell drifted out of the other end of the hall, where the toilet had backed up, but, in spite of this, he headed toward the bathroom. The best thing would be to get on top of the building. He took the stairs in a rush, pushed out the door to the roof, and stumbled into the blinding daylight. After a few seconds, his vision resolved itself into a panorama of Kamaishi's port.

All around him, the city was churning like an enormous machine, breaking down and pumping its pistons a final time. He saw the roof of a nearby house moving. It had just been renovated—the racket from the power tools that had been in his ears for weeks had ceased only days before—but now the water picked the home up whole, carried it a couple blocks, and smashed the structure into a light pole. Smoke and dust filled the sky, and the din of the destruction was like the thunder of artillery. A river had formed in the street, sweeping up everything in its flow: overturned boats, aluminum cans, newspapers, cigarette packs, even a pair of plastic slippers bobbed in the water. In front of a bank a couple hundred yards away, on the roof of a stalled truck, a construction worker and a Buddhist monk in his robes watched the torrent in a daze. It seemed impossible they'd ever get down.

At first, the sound of the disaster had been deafening, but soon Keitaro heard someone shouting through the roar, and, on the roof behind him, he saw a man on the roof of the M apartment building. He recognized his neighbor Maekawa, though he wasn't dressed in the uniform of the security company he worked for.

"Help me!" Maekawa was yelling.

Keitaro's building and the M apartments stood against one another, and it was no trouble for him to scramble over. When he got there and looked down over the edge of the roof where his neighbor was pointing, he saw that one of the city buses had been swept up against the apartment complex.

Six people were struggling to stay afloat in the water around the vehicle. When they saw Maekawa and him they swam back to the bus, climbed onto the roof, and began to shout and wave, animated by their desperation. Their presence jolted Keitaro out of his shock.

"Old man! Old man!" they yelled at him.

He could see several of the passengers were older than he was, and it surprised him to hear this. He didn't see himself the way they must have—the hard, round paunch that had formed over his midsection, the way the bottom of his chin had swollen in affirmation of his late-middle age. He knew he wasn't young anymore, but he'd never thought of himself as old.

"Hey, hey," his neighbor stood next to him at the edge of the roof and yelled down at the stranded commuters. Maekawa talked casually, as if the commuters were friends he'd seen in the supermarket: "Hold on a moment."

Keitaro followed his gaze, looking for any means to help the passengers, until they both spotted a clothesline suspended between two metal poles on the roof of Keitaro's building. Without saying anything, they jogged over and untied the cord. As they returned to the side of the M apartment building, the adrenalin was pulsing through Keitaro, blurring everything.

He wasn't quite sure what he'd hoped for, but, after they threw one end of the line down, it was clear there was no way the two of them could pull these people up. Staring down at the survivors from the bus, he began to see them as individuals: there was a high school student still in his school uniform, four middle-aged women, and a man whose tie, navy blazer, and matching hat marked him as the bus' driver. It was this man who'd caught the cord and was holding one end of it while his neighbor gripped the other. Tenuous though it was, this connection reassured them all in some way—it was better than the hopeless gap that'd been between them before.

By this point, only the roof of the bus was visible, as if it was afloat on the ocean. But the hulking vehicle wasn't moving: despite the charging water, it seemed stable for the moment. The passengers and the driver's clothes were soaked, and before long they began calling out: "We're cold, we're cold."

"I'll get you something," Keitaro said, thinking of the blankets and sheets in his apartment. "Hang on."

He went back to his own roof, retracing his steps down the stairwell into his building. Inside, the space he knew so well had been transformed: with the power out it was dark, he felt an unfamiliar grit beneath his feet, and the stink of the overflowing toilet washed over him as he hurried down the hall. He just hoped his rooms weren't flooded.

When he reached his apartment, the floor was slick, but the shelves where he kept his bed things had been soaked. He grabbed as many sheets and blankets as he could carry and headed back up.

Still holding the cord, his neighbor watched as Keitaro scurried across the roof. When he reached Maekawa, they weren't sure how to get the blankets down to the bus at first.

They decided to tie the blankets around the clothesline and, working together, the neighbors secured the bedding and slid it down to the freezing survivors. He watched as the women, the boy, and the bus driver draped the blankets over their sopping outer layers; these coverings would give them little warmth. They needed to get out of their wet clothes, but they were shy rural people—even an act of God couldn't compel them to undress in public.

They'd done all they could for the stranded bus survivors, and soon Keitaro became aware of another group a few roofs over. They seemed to have come from the Japan Agriculture Bank branch, and there were six of them: a man dressed in a dark suit and five women in matching skirts and vests. They wore indoor sandals, as if they'd rushed away from their desks for a fire drill and would be going back before long. That he'd never met these people, despite how close they'd worked to his salon, was a strange fact of the order that had existed before the tsunami and ceased to matter the moment the waves struck.

The two neighbors made their way to Keitaro's roof and then crossed over onto the adjoining building, which had housed a vegetable market and stood next to the JA Bank branch. Though his neighbor, the bank employees, and he wanted to gather in one place, there was a gap of more than a yard between the buildings. A decent jump might've crossed the span, but everyone was too rattled to try anything like that.

"Is there a desk you could bring up?" Keitaro asked, thinking they could use the office furniture as a bridge.

The bank employees agreed there was probably something that could work, though they seemed reluctant to go back in the building and look. Two of their coworkers had drowned in the tsunami—one of them a twenty-year-old girl who'd just celebrated her coming-of-age ceremony in January. Her body was still below.

Eventually, two of the young women and the well-dressed man went back inside, and several minutes later they reappeared on the stairs, huffing and carrying a long table they'd found in a meeting room. A waist-high chain-link fence bordered the grocery store's roof, and Maekawa and Keitaro each swung one leg over, so that they straddled the barrier. With their help, the JA employees managed to lay the table across the gap.

The first woman who stepped forward to make the crossing was pale and young and pretty. Her plastic sandals clacked against the wood as she stepped onto the surface. She took her first deliberate steps, looking down at her feet and past them into the narrow shaft, which was flooded with dark sludge and half-buried in shadow. Having come a couple shaky meters, she'd just started to consider the drop when the neighbors each grabbed one of her hands and pulled her across—she was over the gap, clinging to the chain-link fence before she knew it.

In this way, the bank employees came over one by one, until everyone was standing on top of the green grocer's building. As Maekawa, Keitaro, and the JA group came back to the roof above his salon, he noticed that the sky had darkened a shade, though he had no idea how long it'd been since he'd come up; it was as if the disaster had washed him to a place outside of time altogether. But when he checked on the bus, he saw the tsunami was retreating: a mess of fishing nets and buoys floated back out to sea, pulled by the current.

Once the water was down near the bus' tires, he told the survivors on its roof to come to Hair Studio K as soon as they could, directing them around to the front entrance. Then, returning to his roof, he led his neighbor and the JA employees down into his building. A few minutes later, the six survivors from the bus joined them in the cramped salon.

Keitaro dragged his old hulking kerosene heater into the middle of the dim room and flicked on the pilot light. Silence held for a few minutes, but, as the air grew warm, the survivors began to talk. The women from the bus all spoke in a thick dialect, and he realized they were from Otsuchi, the community next to Kamaishi, where the bus must have been coming from. He'd always thought that town was rougher than Kamaishi, but, sitting shoulder-to-shoulder with the bus passengers, this idea turned to dust and was replaced by the fact of their individuality. Though everyone in the room had been shaken by what they'd been through, they shared a collective relief now that they were together.

Without power or cell service they had only each other, and among themselves they wondered how far inland the waves had swept, how much of the city had been destroyed, and if anyone would come help them. Of course, no one was coming. Out of Kamaishi's nearly forty-thousand residents, over a thousand were dead or missing. The city's coastline was shattered, the entire region in chaos.

As the sun set, the survivors began to consider what they should do next. They decided to walk to Kamaishi Elementary School, one of the city's designated evacuation areas. The streets were clogged with debris, so Keitaro set about finding shoes for the JA employees; they'd never manage the trek in their sandals. It took a couple trips back and forth from his rooms, but soon the bank employees were outfitted in his boots and tennis shoes. His footwear clashed with the bank employees uniforms, but they would make do.

The group of fourteen survivors filed out of the salon. Keitaro took the small pack with his scissors and other tools and carried it with him as he headed down the wet stairs.

Outside, the day's light was dying, the streets were blacked with mud, and their group seemed to be walking through the bottom of the evening's dark. They had a couple of flashlights from Keitaro's room, and those who'd kept their cell phones dry used them as lights. Their route to the school took them past where the waves had swept the bus up against the buildings on Keitaro's block; seen from the street the vehicle appeared bigger, though the mud encrusted on it and the wreckage jutting through where the windows had been made it almost unrecognizable. Looking more closely, he realized what he'd mistaken for debris were two pairs of lifeless legs.

After that, Keitaro kept his head down as he walked, carefully avoiding looking at the details of the desolation, aware that he was surrounded by death. This was easy enough; the day had been a series of shocks that had pushed him past his limits again and again, and though he knew grief should have been overcoming him, he felt only fatigue, exhaustion seeping into his very bones.

Trudging through the mud and navigating the heaped ruins, their group made slow progress. A walk that normally took five minutes would wind up dragging on for over twenty. A dusting of snow had begun to shake out of the sky, laying a thin blanket of white over the wreckage-strewn streets. Keitaro watched his shuffling feet as, for the first time in hours, his thoughts turned again to his mother.

II. The Hills Above, the Sea Below

Otsuchi Town, Iwate Prefecture
When it started, Jun Akazaki was putting the café in order, the TV playing in the background.

His mother and he had a coffee shop in the back of the first floor of their building, and he also ran a rice store out of the front. On the second floor, there was a Buddhist shrine for Jun's late father and a small office for their businesses. On the third floor, his mother and he each had a bedroom, and from the roof they had a view of Otsuchi's shopping district, the town's quiet port in the distance.

That afternoon, his mother had invited a few friends from her haiku poetry circle over to eat, have coffee, and admire the display of dolls she'd put out for Girl's Day. Every year for the Hinamatsuri, she set out a seven-step platform showcasing figurines that represented the ancient Heian court: the Emperor and Empress in flowing kimonos at the top, court ladies pouring sake below, then the wise, gray-haired ministers, and the musicians clutching miniature flutes and tiny *taiko* drums. Once every two years, she held a party and served her friends bowls of red bean rice and clam soup in honor of the holiday. Her guests were coming at 4:00 p.m., but at 2:45 p.m. the ground gave a shudder.

When the first tremor hit, Jun froze, the trembling fixing him in place. The china cups and saucers quivered on their shelves, and then the refrigerator and tables and chairs and every piece of furniture in his café—so silent before—began to rattle and shake. There'd been a small quake a couple days before, but nothing like this: as if the earth itself was growling.

After several minutes, the vibrations started to die out, and, in the quiet that followed, he knew, though the swell would probably be a small one—at worst it might do some damage to the old, rusting fishing boats down at the docks—they should evacuate. He started up the stairs to the second floor, to his mother.

Jun had spent nearly all his life in Otsuchi. He'd been born in the area in 1964 and attended high school in Kamaishi, the next city over. He'd gone away to Sendai for college, but after earning a degree in economics from Tohoku Gakuin University, he'd come back and taken over his family's rice shop and Mumins, the café his mother had started. Growing up, he'd heard about tsunamis that had devastated the region in the past.

He found his mother in the room that held his father's shrine, which they also used when they had company. Her dolls had fallen from the platform and she was picking them up.

"What? Everything's fine," she said, looking at him.

"We have to go," he told her.

"We're not in any danger here."

"A wave could come."

Jun moved around his mother, flicked off the space heater, and went after her down the stairs. The initial quiet that had followed the quake was turning into a cacophony of noise: doors and windows slammed shut, cars sped through the streets, people shouted to be heard. On his way out, he turned off the heater on the first floor—a precaution he'd later be glad he'd remembered—grabbed a jacket, took a ten-thousand-yen bill from the rice shop's register, and stuffed it in his pocket. Five minutes had passed since the earthquake.

Outside, everything was panic and flight. The narrow road in front of their building was jammed with cars as people tried to get to the evacuation areas. Jun and his mother owned a light truck, and she went to the passenger side of the cab. He lowered the metal shutters over their storefronts, as if he was closing shop for the day. He was about to get in the driver's seat when he saw one of his neighbors. The old man lived next door and was standing in the brisk air watching the exodus.

"Let's go," Jun said, motioning him over. "Come with us."

"My daughter is on her way. I'll wait for her."

In his haste, Jun didn't think to argue with him. As with many of the people he saw in those final, confused minutes, it would be the last time he ever saw his neighbor, who'd lived next to him for more than ten years.

Jun slid behind the truck's wheel, twisting the key in the ignition. He shifted into gear and pulled into the alley behind their place, which let out onto Highway 45, the main route through town. Everyone was heading right toward the Shiroyama Community Center, a cluster of buildings on a tall foothill in the middle of Otsuchi; it was only a short drive away, but the road had become a traffic snarl. He turned left, took another left at the next stoplight, and then another after the park on the next block, navigating a semicircle through the narrow streets—a back way to the Koganji temple grounds.

The temple lay at the bottom of the same rise that the community center stood atop, not even half a kilometer as the crow flies from their building. A graveyard beside the temple covered the hill beside the main hall, and a walkway snaked up the terraced levels of stone monuments. At the top of the path, on the other side of a knee-high imitation-wood fence, was the community center. They'd be out of any danger there.

He parked in the temple's gravel lot. Getting out of the truck, Jun and his mother passed between the towering beams of the gate, heading for the courtyard, which was already crowded. He thought he might recognize some of the evacuees if he had a moment, but, while he'd initially seen their flight as a precaution, the frenzied atmosphere was heightening his sense of alarm. His mother started up the hill, and he said he'd be right behind.

He watched her walk toward the very graveyard where his father and grandfather's bones were interred; she was the only parent he had left, and his love for her was immense. Years ago, he'd reconciled himself to the life of a bachelor. He would never marry, never start a family. Instead, he had his band Mumins, which he played in with four middle-age friends and had named after the café; he had his other musician friends in the area and the handful of drinking establishments where he was a regular. These connections sustained him. No one would have mistaken Otsuchi for a posh neighborhood in Tokyo, but here he was content.

As he stood outside the temple, where he came every year to make a New Year's offering, he saw the town's elderly going into the main hall. Many of them didn't move well and were cold in the freezing March air as they shuffled between the entrance's white concrete pillars. Still, this seemed insane.

He spotted a man he knew from the neighborhood and, though he couldn't remember his name, went to him saying, "Wouldn't it be better to get them up the hill?"

There were a few people who agreed with him, but many of the older people couldn't be convinced to try to go up the hill. Jun stayed there, arguing for taking the elders up into the heights of the graveyard for several minutes, before he heard the people above him calling out: "Come on, come on. Quick!"

He started up the path, taking the walkway as fast as he could. He stopped when he found his mother, a little more than halfway up the trail. From there, the sounds of evacuation were distant, and the town spread out below them: traffic moved slowly on Route 45, and farther off the bay's blue-gray v cut into the coastal plain, where most of Otsuchi's buildings were bunched together. From the hillside, through the clear, crisp air, the town looked so tranquil. Around them, grave markers covered the hillside. Each granite gravestone had a pillar where a surname was carved; behind the markers, tall wooden boards painted with the names of individual family members stood in stone receptacles. At the base of the hill lay the red-tile roof of the temple's main hall, where the elderly who couldn't make it up the hill had taken shelter.

As Jun and his mother caught their breath, the others who'd taken shelter on the hill began calling for those below to come up. He added his voice to theirs saying, "It's safer up here."

On the hill, everyone was excited and talking all at once, especially the children—the schools had been sure to evacuate—and it seemed there were more kids in the hills than adults. His mother stared at the bay: the surface of the ocean was striped with bands of whitewater as surges raced toward Otsuchi. The districts nearest the shore were already flooded, and black cubes floated in the current, which he now realized were cars. From that point on, the higher the water rose, the more he felt he was being sucked into a lucid nightmare.

The tsunami didn't take the form of one huge curling wave but was more like a very quick flood. The flow rushed into the cleft of the Otsuchi River first—the concrete-lined banks filled with ashen water as if the channel was a bowl set under a gushing tap. A surge rubbed out a dark line that spanned the river, washing away the bridge that carried the Yamada local train. The tsunami slammed the districts on the far side of the port, sending up plumes of dust like a Hollywood special effect. Water cascaded over the river's banks and rushed toward where Jun's building was. The sheet-metal roofs of the structures nearest the coast shook and fell out of view as waves flattened them. Concrete power poles snapped like pieces of straw. Jun had thought a tsunami might come, but he'd never imagined anything like this.

At first, the carnage had been remote, muted, but as the water advanced, the roar of destruction rose all around him. The children's exclamations turned to screams, as if they weren't sure if they should be thrilled or upset. One boy cried, "I'll never forget you, father," a girl said, "My home, my home," while others simply screamed "*Yabai.*" How terrible.

A man above him said, "Look. Those people." When Jun peered into the pattern of buildings, he saw a car and a motorcycle come flying around a corner—then several people on foot, sprinting for their lives as a black flow of debris spilled into the street behind them. The vehicles outran the water and disappeared behind a roofline. Most of the runners made it out of sight, though the last few were swallowed by the waves.

Through it all, Jun had kept an eye on his home. His father had overseen the construction of their building in 1988, had called the contractors and made the plans himself—it was his last remaining material legacy. But, as Jun watched, a veil of brown dust covered his view. What he could see were birds: tens, maybe hundreds of crows and seagulls stirred from their perches by the chaos. They took flight, leaving Otsuchi behind with such ease.

He could also still see the temple's main hall below. He saw the water crash into it, breaking down the front door. In seconds, the flood was up past the windows. Jun knew there must've been thirty-or-forty people inside. It was a mercy when a cloud of dust concealed the sight.

In the three minutes he'd been standing there, the tsunami had destroyed more than half of his hometown. Beside him, his mother was crying, and none of it felt real. He'd fled as a precaution, but he'd been sure he would be back in his café before long. It seemed at any minute he might find himself brewing a cup of coffee, talking with a customer about a strange dream: a vision of the world underwater and the town full of the dead and the living in a graveyard. And yet he remained on the hillside cemetery. Each minute he stood there, reality diverged further and further from this image.

It took a while for the dust to dissipate. When it did, Jun and his mother saw their building was still standing, the tops of the second-floor windows just visible above the water. He couldn't tell how badly it had been damaged, and many of the other structures that were still upright looked ruined; the town's hospital hadn't collapsed but was battered like a beaten prizefighter about to pitch over.

Hours passed as the tsunami gradually receded—the flooding would ebb, but then another surge would push inland, and time seemed to stretch and compress, changing with the speed and direction of the currents. It was still light when a small group decided to go and look for survivors.

"I'm going with them," Jun told his mother.

At the base of the hill, the ground was buried in a layer of wreckage: broken cinder blocks, dented propane tanks, over-turned refrigerators, crushed TV sets, all the things that make up houses, stores, factories, but smashed to pieces and mixed together, as if the entire town had been puréed in a giant blender and poured out. Jun climbed through the remains, every step a venture that might land on a hidden nail or piece of torn metal. Crawling through what was left of Otsuchi was exhausting, and he was terrified that another wave would surge into the ruins and sweep him out to sea. He looked for his truck but couldn't even pick out the place where he'd parked.

He hadn't gone far when he heard a cry, a whisper almost. "*Tasukete, tasukete.*" Help, help.

"We're coming," he said, hurrying forward on all fours.

When he reached where the voice had come from, he began digging. His hands were so cold he barely noticed scraping them on the splintered boards he tossed aside. At the bottom of the rubble was a woman's face, dirty and dark and bruised. With the help of the other searchers, Jun carefully dragged her from the refuse and carried her up the hill.

The survivors who weren't helping search tended to the woman, and Jun went back down. With the few other able-bodied evacuees, he helped pull three more from the wreckage. One old man moaned as they carried him up the path, and he died just minutes later.

Another of those they pulled from the wreckage was Ryokan Ogayu, one of the sons of the family of priests that had ministered at Koganji Temple for generations. Though his brother had managed to pull himself from the wreckage, Ryokan had barely kept himself from drowning. One of the other searchers discovered him and called out for help digging him out.

Jun pitched in, and, together, they managed to get Ryokan on a soaked woven-straw *tatami* mat someone had found in the wreckage. The priest looked as though he'd been spun inside a washing machine: he'd lost his glasses and his clothes were wet and disheveled. He was a heavy man, and it took several people to pull him up the hill.

Jun kept searching until it grew dark. Then, in the dusk, he retreated up the hill. From there, he saw the fires. The blazes were multiplying, weaving a burning orange pattern through the dark buildings and sending up shadowy ribbons of smoke. Looking at the landscape was like staring into the dying embers in a wood stove; a flare might be a gas line exploding in the distance, a pulsating knot of heat might be the dry goods store.

At some point, it had started to snow. Soon he would walk with his mother to the top of the hill, climb over the guardrail, and retreat into the community center's gym. They wouldn't be able to get any rest, and it would be days before the sense of shock wore off; soon they'd need to start worrying about where they'd sleep at night, where they'd find their next meal. Eventually, they'd try to forget what they'd seen, let it fade like a childhood fear of the dark, until it was a memory unable to reach them other than to send a shiver down their backs now and again. In the months and years to come, they'd put it behind them because they had to, because they needed to keep moving, keep living, letting one day follow the next.

But, in that moment, he and his mother looked on, transfixed by the fires spreading among the shredded debris. Neither of them spoke as an arm of flame moved across the night, closing in on their home.

Nuclear Shocks

March 2011

I. Nuclear Family

Okuma Town, Fukushima Prefecture

Tsuneo Sakai was inside reactor building three at the Fukushima Daiichi nuclear power plant when the shaking started. In each of the reactor buildings, a complex network of pipes fed water into the reactor, where super-heated fuel rods turned it to steam and forced it out of a different set of pipes, sending the gas to the turbine building where it spun enormous fan blades, generating hundreds of megawatts of electricity each day. That day, a Friday, the third reactor was shut down, and Tsuneo's team was at work on the building's plumbing.

Tsuneo was holding a pipe steady while another worker used a metal grinder to carve it open. With the vibrating metal under his hands and the whine of the cutting in his ears, at first, he didn't notice the quake—by the time he felt the shaking, the floor was heaving beneath his feet.

The rest of the men had also felt the vibrations and stopped working as tremors rocked the room. The pipe Tsuneo had been holding was anchored to the ceiling by metal supports, but as it rattled, the metal collars holding it in place bent until they seemed about to break. The glass of the overhead lights cracked, and then the room vanished into darkness. The earthquake rolled on in the black and he could hardly stand.

After the tremors died away, a quiet moment followed. The power was out. Gone was the screech of power tools, the sound of his team's work; even the reactor, which usually emitted a low hum, hinting at the incredible forces it contained, was silent. After several minutes, one of the building's safety officers turned on a flashlight, cutting open the dark. This security guard told them to evacuate, but Tsuneo waited until his boss, Aita-*san*, gave the order: "Let's get the hell out of here."

Leaving their tools, they filed out of the reactor building as the tsunami warning sirens blasted throughout the plant. It was near three in the afternoon and they usually got off at five; with the power out, there was no way they'd return to work that day. But all Tsuneo was thinking of was getting home, back to the apartment he shared with his mother and their cat.

Outside, in the bright day, he saw where the quake had broken open fissures in the roads that crisscrossed the plant. When he looked toward the ocean, the tide was out.

Around him, maintenance personnel and staff from reactors three and four were streaming outside. The paths between the buildings bustled with people. It seemed like confusion, but all the personnel knew their duties in case of emergency. Tsuneo wasn't a TEPCO employee, but he worked for Tokyo Energy Systems as a subcontractor; he and his team were supposed to report to their office on the plant's grounds. The building was over a kilometer away. A bus took them to their jobsite each morning and picked them up in the afternoon, but no one was coming for them now. Aita, the team leader, began walking, and then Tsuneo followed with the rest of the men.

When they reached the office, they joined a scrum of hundreds of plumbers, welders, and other workers. One of the managers was checking everyone's name off against a list to make sure they'd all made it back.

By the time Tsuneo's name was called and he was given the okay to leave, he couldn't wait to get away. After a shake like that, he figured a tsunami would come. He didn't want to be around when it arrived.

Though he'd never worried for his safety when working at the plant, now doubt began to creep into his mind. The plant's wave wall was low, and for years the company had put off safety measures, like moving the diesel emergency generators out of the basement.

He was searching the crowd for Ando-*san*, the man whom he carpooled into work with every day. With each passing minute, the situation became more desperate and tangled; tsunami sirens kept sounding, and, by the time he looked at his cell phone, the network was down. Cars were streaming out of the plant as hundreds of TEPCO employees fled, leaving behind a skeleton crew to run the emergency response center.

Finally, Tsuneo found Ando and the other men from Okuma whom he'd driven in with. Barely a word passed between them as they went to the parking lot, piled in the car, and drove away from Fukushima Daiichi. Tsuneo had no idea it would be the last time he'd set foot on the plant's grounds for years to come.

Theirs was one of many vehicles fleeing, and, soon, the traffic slowed to a crawl. Up ahead, cars were turning around and speeding back the other direction. As they inched forward, Tsuneo saw the road was broken. The ground had sunk, and the asphalt had cracked like a sheet of black ice; some pieces of blacktop were lifted high in the air while others had fallen into a kind of sinkhole. Crevasses of fresh brown dirt yawned open between the chucks of pavement.

In the morning, he'd thought nothing of it when they'd driven over this same stretch of road. But as Ando turned the car around, and Tsuneo tried to remember which back roads they could use to reach Okuma, the certainties of his life were splitting open like the asphalt of the road—the stability of the plant, the safety of his home, these were question marks now. The highway was the main link between the towns along the coast.

If it was impassable, there was no telling what roads were open. There was no knowing how he'd get back, or if he even would.

Earlier that afternoon, Tsuneo's mother, Katsue Sakai, had been at the Original Salon getting a perm. She'd finished sitting under the dryer hood and was in a salon chair, looking at a magazine as her hair cooled. The stylist, an older woman whom Katsue always came to, was in the back with her daughter, waiting for Katsue's hair to finish drying before she took the rollers out.

Katsue sat next to a vanity mirror with a shelf filled with dryers, curlers, straighteners, and other hair appliances. One electric cord hung down from the shelf in front of the glass, and Katsue noticed it moving slightly. Her eyes weren't what they used to be, and she squinted. Was the cord swaying or was it the light playing a trick on her?

At fifty-four, Katsue wasn't young. Still, she took care of herself, and she'd come to the salon because of Okuma's upcoming election. In the past, she'd worked as an announcer for local politicians, and there was a new candidate running for local representative. She would drive around with him in the campaign car, and, while he waved to voters, she would speak into a microphone, politely encouraging them to vote for him, adding a feminine touch to the campaign. This was just one of the many jobs Katsue had pursued. She may not have been a girl anymore, but she'd found plenty to keep her busy.

This was why, when she realized that not only was the cord moving, but so was the vanity and the wall and the chair beneath her, she didn't want to mess up her perm, didn't want to interrupt her busy schedule. But the quake intensified, knocking bottles of hairspray, shampoo, and coloring off the shelves. Katsue stumbled out of the chair and lurched for the door, the stylist and her daughter on her heels.

Outside, the three women watched the buildings rock, the parked cars bobbing on their springs. Several minutes went by before the shaking stilled.

The stylist turned to Katsue and said, "You'd better go."

"Like this?" Katsue asked. The rollers were still in her hair.

"I can't do anything as it is." Inside, beauty products littered the floor. The power was off.

"But I haven't paid," Katsue said.

"Later is fine."

In any case, Katsue was worried; besides her son, her little black and white cat was the closest member of her family. Coo was small and not as spry as she'd been as a kitten. Trapped in the apartment, she could've been crushed under the TV or a falling shelf.

Katsue got in her car, started it up, and pulled into the road. She didn't make it far before she reached a place where the asphalt had cracked; the ground had pushed up on one side, forming a step too high for her Honda to get over. She turned around and tried other roads until she found a passable route. By the time she parked in the lot between the two tower blocks of the public housing complex and took the stairs to the third floor, all she could think of was Coo. She reached the top floor, turned her key in the lock, and threw open the apartment door.

Within the mess—the shoe shelf had fallen, spilling her and Tsuneo's footwear across the entry—Coo was in a corner, curled into a shaking ball.

Katsue went inside as relief spread through her. She found Coo's carrier and coaxed the cat inside. Then Katsue went to the bathroom, took the curlers out of her hair, and washed out the perm solution. Afterward, she started picking up the apartment. She was still straightening the rooms when the first aftershock hit.

The building began to sway—on the third floor, it was as if she was on a ship rolling between enormous swells.

She grabbed Coo's carrier, hurrying out the door and down the stairs. In the parking area on the ground floor, she waited out the tremors with Coo. Once the rumbling faded, she thought of going back up, but she'd also started to wonder about her son.

She figured Tsuneo would be on his way home, but it had been an hour since the quake. The nuclear plant was only ten minutes away. Sitting and worrying wouldn't accomplish anything though, so she put Coo in the passenger seat of her Honda and went back up to clean a little, before the next aftershock sent her racing downstairs again. Several times, she went up to the apartment only to rush out when the building began to shudder.

It was past four and she was huddling in a corner on the ground floor when, finally, the company car Tsuneo had left in that morning pulled into the parking lot. Her son climbed out the back; he had Katsue's dark features, her small frame. He was just past thirty and had been with her his entire life. To say she was happy to see him would have been like saying she was happy for the air she breathed; he was her beautiful boy and she could never imagine being without him.

But she didn't say this. Instead, as the company car drove off, she told him Coo had been scared, their apartment was a mess, the aftershocks had terrified her. It would be night soon, and they went to take a last look at the apartment, but there was little they could do in the near dark.

With her son and Coo safe, Katsue had started to wonder how her friends were managing. She decided they should check on the couple who ran Daikatsu Diner, where Katsue had been going to since she was a girl. Though Oi-*san* and his wife had a daughter of their own, they'd always looked after Katsue as if she were family. She'd eaten so many plates of Daikatsu noodles—their signature vegetable and pork *yakisoba*—she'd lost count.

She got in the passenger side of the Honda, and Tsuneo drove them west on Okuma's main road until they saw the big, white two-story house attached to the restaurant. Tsuneo parked and Katsue went to the door. Katsuo Oi answered looking strained and exhausted, though he immediately invited them inside. The power was out there too.

Daikatsu Diner had been open for business as usual in the afternoon. Katsuo and his wife had finished with lunch and were prepping for dinner when the earthquake hit, plunging the kitchen into darkness. Without power or gas, they couldn't cook or serve customers, so they'd scooped out the rice in their industrial-sized cooker and shaped it into rice balls. Now, they offered these to Katsue and Tsuneo.

After eating, they moved to the living room, which was dominated by an enormous *kotatsu*, a low table with a blanket that hung down from the sides to trap the heat. Knowing Katsue and Tsuneo wouldn't have electricity or gas at home, Katsuo's wife entreated them: "Just stay here."

Katsue quickly agreed. All of them had been shaken by the quake, and the sense of togetherness was reassuring. When Katsue mentioned Coo out in the car, Katsuo's wife said they should bring the little darling in. Katsue went out, got the carrier, and released Coo inside the house so she could wind her way around the unfamiliar rooms, slinking between the legs of the chairs and tables.

Eventually, Katsue, Tsuneo, Katsuo, and his wife all settled at the *kotatsu*. As the night deepened, each of them took a side of the table and did their best to sleep. They tried to avoid each other's feet as they woke with the aftershocks, which rumbled over the town like passing storms.

March 12

Just before six in the morning, Katsue heard one of the patrol cars that had been dispatched by the town blaring an official message through the neighborhood: "All residents are advised to keep doors and windows closed. Please stay indoors. All residents are advised to keeps door and windows closed..."

What was this about? She felt uneasy, but she'd never been the type to blindly follow orders. She decided to take a peek outside. Stepping out the front door, she looked down the road that passed in front of the diner, toward the intersection with the highway. In the morning's weak light, a handful of figures in protective suits milled about at the corner, taking measurements of she didn't know what. Though she had no idea what they were doing, the sight of them gave her a strange feeling. She went inside.

After breakfasting on rice balls left from the night before, Katsue and Tsuneo thanked Katsuo and his wife. The older couple had decided to go south to Gunma Prefecture to stay with a relative. Katsue couldn't think of imposing on their kindness any further, and, with the worst of the aftershocks over, she planned on returning home.

As Tsuneo drove them back to their apartment, she noticed the traffic flowing west, and when they pulled into the public housing complex, there were few cars left in the lot. Still, without knowing what was going on, all she and Tsuneo could do was to get their apartment in order.

They parked and went upstairs. In the daylight, she noticed the pans and dishes scattered all over the kitchen. She picked them up and thought to wash them, but when she turned the faucet there was no water in the pipes. She left the dishes and helped her son pick up the things that had fallen and moved them to the side or the corners, clearing the floor. Still, there was only so much they could do without power or water.

Katsue wasn't the type to sit on her hands though. She'd worked her way through every calamity in life. When her first marriage had gone south—she'd met her husband while working in a hospital in Tokyo, after graduating from nursing school in the city—she'd moved back to Okuma and found work in her hometown. Tsuneo had been only three at the time, but her parents had looked after him while she was at the hospital. She took time off when she got pregnant again—the result of another relationship that hadn't lasted—but after her daughter was born, Katsue went right back to work and found a new nursing position at Kosei Hospital in Futaba, the next town over. She worked in the surgery department for two decades and also started moonlighting at a local drinking establishment called Hibiki, owned by an older woman named Masako Iida and her husband. Katsue served cocktails and chatted with the local men who came to drink and sing *enka* songs on the karaoke machine.

And so, with the disaster over, having done all they could in their apartment, she didn't wait around for the power to come on or the water to return. She decided they would have to go down to the river to wash the dishes that had fallen.

Tsuneo drove them to the Kuma River, though no one was out on the road. The sky was starting to darken as they walked down to the bank, where the water ran past in a clear flow. They were crouched on the bank, leaning over the current to polish their plates and pans, when a voice called out to them.

"What are you doing?"

Looking, Katsue saw a man in the fire station's uniform. He'd been sent to tell people to evacuate, he explained, and was going around making sure no one was left behind. The danger of radiation, trouble at the nuclear plant—these thoughts hadn't entered her mind, and so when she asked the firefighter where they were supposed to go, she was surprised at his urgency.

"Just head west," he said. "Take the highway toward Koriyama."

That was all he said before turning and running off. As she and Tsuneo trudged up the bank and back to the Honda, she was beginning to panic.

There was no telling what was happening at the nuclear plant. Unsure, she told Tsuneo to drive to the house of the Yoshidas, a couple whom she was friendly with.

Their house was only a couple of minutes away, and Katsue and Tsuneo found them preparing to flee their house—like all the residents of Okuma, they were leaving almost everything behind. After a brief chat, the four of them agreed to head west together on the highway. They had no choice.

In their flight, all she and Tsuneo took were a few dishes and Coo and her carrier in the backseat. Katsue had about 2,000 yen on her, not even enough for a hotel room.

Tsuneo drove west on local roads until they merged onto Route 288, the national highway. They'd left Okuma behind when they hit a wall of traffic. Katsue realized the cars she'd seen earlier had been full of people with the sense to evacuate at the first sign of trouble. By now, the whole town was on the road. Tsuneo did his best to stick close to the Yoshidas' back bumper, as they climbed into the green foothills separating the coast from Fukushima's inland region. On one side of the road, metal nets guarded against rockslides, while, on the other, a guardrail was all that stood between them and a plunging slope. The sharp switchbacks slowed them, and, in the space that opened up between their Honda and the Yoshidas, other cars merged onto Route 288: all the cities and towns on the coast were emptying out, and vehicles poured onto the highway from smaller roads like water flowing from tributaries into a great river. By the time they crossed over into the neighboring city, they'd lost the Yoshidas in the traffic.

The edge of Tamura City was made up of the Miyakoji District, and, as they searched for a place to stay the night—if they kept driving like this, they'd run out of gas—Katsue thought of Aoki-san, a regular customer who came to Hibiki so often he was practically family. When he'd come to the drinking establishment he'd mentioned that he lived in Miyakoji, and she had his number in her phone. She hadn't noticed when, but her cell service had started working again. Now, she found his contact information and pressed the dial button.

When he picked up, she explained they'd evacuated and were on the road.

"Everyone from Hibiki is already here," Aoki said. "Come on over."

Following his instructions, she told Tsuneo where to turn off the highway and directed him through the local roads, looking for Masako Iida's car in the unfamiliar neighborhood.

It was evening by the time they found Aoki's house and parked. Inside, Masako and her husband, who Katsue had only ever met in the bar and had always called Master, were relieved to see them. For the first time since they'd left Okuma, Katsue felt as though she could take a breath.

It had taken them almost an hour to reach Tamura City, and she figured whatever was happening with the nuclear plant wouldn't reach them there. They could stay the night and plan their next move tomorrow. Aoki brought out tea as Katsue and Tsuneo sat in the living room, talking with the old bar master and his wife. Without cell service, TV, or the time to slow down and listen to the radio, no one knew much about what was going on.

Katsue hadn't decided what she and Tsuneo would do the next day, she hadn't even had time to get Coo from the backseat of their Honda, when the district loudspeakers bleated out a new announcement: the mandatory evacuation zone had been expanded to twenty kilometers. All Miyakoji District residents were ordered to take shelter.

Katsue roused herself. It was ridiculous—they were evacuating *from* the place they'd evacuated to—but what choice did they have? She went with Tsuneo, who got in the car, started it up, and pulled out, joining a new wave of traffic, following the Iidas as closely as he could.

They drove west toward Koriyama, the prefecture's largest city. The problem of where they would stay pressed in on them like the night's darkness. They could sleep in the car, but they needed to reach someplace safe first. In the back, Coo was hunched and silent in her carrier.

After they'd driven a few kilometers out of the district, the Iida's car slowed and signaled for a turn, pulling off the highway and onto a narrow road that took them to the Tamura City Sports Center. Tsuneo turned in behind them, though the parking lot was crowded with cars. The old bar master went in to see if they could stay there, only to come out several minutes later with a resigned look on his face. The place was already full of refugees. They'd given him directions to another shelter he could try down the road, and so their three-car caravan continued west. They repeated this scene at a couple more shelters before finally being directed to a park in Koriyama, where someone would help them find shelter.

The Iidas plugged the address into their car's navigation system, and Aoki, Tsuneo, and Katsue followed them west. When they reached the city, they pulled off the highway and headed for the sports complex at the center of the Kaiseizan Park.

Though Koriyama didn't have a baseball team, Kaiseizan Stadium had hosted professional games in the past, and, after the city hall had been damaged in the earthquake, the city's Disaster Response Center had moved their equipment across the street and set up in the cement halls beneath the grandstands.

They pulled into the stadium's parking lot, and Tsuneo found a space. Getting out, he and Katsue followed Aoki, Masako, and her husband, joining a line of people outside a tent that had been set up in the parking lot. Inside, people in protective clothing were examining evacuees with boxy instruments attached to probes about the size and the shape of flashlights.

When Katsue reached the front of the line and stepped into the tent, she saw her examiner wore a shower cap and plastic smock. He stepped toward Katsue, passing the probe over her head then shoulders, going all the way down to the bottoms of her feet. Katsue had no idea what he was checking for or why she had to go through this. But, after a moment, he waved her through with his latex-gloved hand.

Once she was on the other side of the tent, she found Tsuneo, Aoki, and the Iidas. After they'd given their names to one of the officials and explained their routes of evacuation, they were told to head to Northern Koriyama Industrial High School. There was still space in the gym there. Masako's husband got the address, and they all went back to their cars. Their three vehicles pulled out of the parking lot and drove in formation, heading north through the narrow city streets.

As Katsue rode in the passenger seat of the Honda—Tsuneo behind the wheel beside her and Coo in the back—she felt a sense of relief, knowing there was a place waiting for them.

March 13

Tsuneo woke from the cold and stretched his body out of the cramped position he'd slept in. Though his mother was in the shelter, which was packed with evacuees, he'd decided to spend the night in the car. If he'd wanted, he could've slept inside on one of the blankets provided by the Self-Defense Forces, but pets weren't permitted inside the high school's gymnasium. He couldn't leave Coo by herself and so had taken his rest in the Honda.

The events of the past couple days were like a dream to him. After leaving the plant and finding the highway impassable, he and his coworkers had driven through the hilly back roads and managed to find their way to Okuma.

But since that bit of luck, his situation had gotten worse with every turn. When the firefighter had found him and his mother on the bank of the river and told them to evacuate, Tsuneo realized there was a problem at the plant. The reactors were equipped with cooling systems that were supposed to automatically kick in during an emergency, but if TEPCO was worried about a radiation release then they must have been having trouble getting water to the cores.

How much had he and his mom been exposed to? Would they get sick? No one was telling them anything, and there was no way of knowing for sure. They'd fled to Miyakoji in Tamura City just in time for the evacuation zone to be expanded, putting them back on the road again. The utility obviously didn't have the situation under control.

Tsuneo opened the Honda's door and stepped into the brisk morning. He walked to the gymnasium to get breakfast. A TV had been set up there, and, for the first time in days, he had a chance to watch the news. The announcer said an accident had taken place at the plant the day before, and the broadcast switched to footage that had been shot by camera a kilometer or so from the plant: the white buildings and crane-like exhaust vents stood out against the blue ocean. The scene seemed almost peaceful, and then the Unit One reactor disappeared in a burst into smoke.

Gray clouds drifted off to either side as the announcer reported that the source of the explosion was unknown. Workers were still trying to get water into the reactor's core.

Later, helicopter footage revealed that the roof had blown off Unit One's building, though the rest of the structure appeared intact. If the core had been exposed, it would be the worst civilian nuclear accident in the country's history. The announcer went on to say that the cores of the other reactors might be overheating. The utility had to work fast.

Tsuneo still felt an attachment, a responsibility, to his old jobsite, but there was nothing he could do from the refugee center in Koriyama. Since driving off Fukushima Daiichi's grounds in the company car, he'd rode the tide of calamity and washed up in the parking lot of this high school so far from his home.

The gymnasium was filled with people from towns all over the mandatory evacuation zone: Okuma, Tamura, Futaba, Kawauchi. Other than the gym, Northern Koriyama Industrial High consisted of four long, rectangular classroom buildings connected by enclosed passageways. Behind the building was a pool and, beside it, a dirt soccer field, where the local kids came to play.

Tsuneo was glad for the shelter and the food. The women who usually made the school lunch had taken on the responsibility of cooking for the evacuees, and when Tsuneo and his mother had arrived the night before, they'd eaten their first hot meal in days. It was simple fare: rice and miso soup, side dishes made from tinned fish or whatever emergency provisions were available. But to them, it had been a delicious.

For the moment, he was more than happy to find in his mother among the evacuees, take another bowl of warm rice, and chat with Masako and her husband as they listened for news about the plant. Still, he couldn't keep an uneasy feeling from creeping into the back of his mind.

March 14

On Monday, just like the day before, Tsuneo and his mother were in the gymnasium, talking with the other evacuees from Okuma after breakfast when the TV announcer interrupted the broadcast, saying there was an update from the nuclear plant. A small crowd formed around the screen as the video feed switched to a faraway shot of the plant, the squat reactor buildings.

Tsuneo could just pick out the third reactor building, where he and his team had been working three days before. He knew once the TEPCO personnel got the reactor cooled, workers from Tokyo Energy Systems would probably have to check all the plumbing in the buildings—and then the third reactor exploded.

The blast shook the camera. Unlike the detonation of the Unit One reactor, this time the smoke shot straight up, as if a bomb had hit the building. A dark-gray mushroom cloud billowed up twice as high as the exhaust towers, blanketing the plant in radioactive material.

Later, Tsuneo would see aerial footage of the building. Unlike with the previous explosion, this blast had completely destroyed the third reactor's containment building. At the time, and for years later, it wasn't exactly clear what had caused the blast; the damaged reactors were too hot with radiation for any machine, let alone person, to get a look at the core. Yet, neither TEPCO nor Prime Minister Kan's administration would use the word meltdown; just a few hours after the Unit Three explosion, Yukio Edano, the Chief Cabinet Secretary, went on TV and claimed there had been no significant release of radiation.

Like most of the evacuees, Tsuneo couldn't tell what to make of all this. What he did know was that there was no longer a job for him to return to. The cloud from the blast hadn't just enveloped the nuclear plant, but the future of his hometown as well. As he watched the news, he was beginning to realize that his and his mother's lives had changed in an instant. Their troubles were only just beginning.

II. The Contamination of Yoshizawa Ranch

Minami-Souma City and Namie Town, Fukushima Prefecture

Masami Yoshizawa had driven half an hour up the coast from his ranch to pick up a few cans of spray paint in Minami-Souma. Coming from Namie, the small city's crisscrossing power lines, close-set buildings, and signs advertising car dealerships, gas stations, and a Sapporo-style ramen shop seemed almost urban.

He found a spot in the Cainz Home parking lot and switched off his two-ton Isuzu's engine. His truck was like an extension of his body and he drove it everywhere; he could haul cattle and feed in the hydraulic bed, lift fallen branches or even small trees with the winch. Climbing out, he headed for the home improvement center's entrance. When he walked his eyes were half-closed, and he seemed to look without seeing. He'd worked with livestock for years—nudging heifers into pens and shoving the heads of curious calves away from tractor wheels—and he'd taken on an oblivious, almost animal way of moving.

Inside the store, fluorescent light bounced off the polished tile floor and pop music trickled through the background. He took a plastic basket from a stack next to the automatic doors and, a few minutes later, was wandering an aisle between two tall shelves, several cans of spray paint rolling back and forth in his carrier. And then the quake struck.

The first vibration might've been a shiver running down his spine, but soon he realized the whole store was shaking. The towering shelves swayed, tracing wider and wider arcs through the air. A convulsion from deep in the ground seized the building, sending fry pans, plastic buckets, dog food bags, and bottles of window cleaner crashing to the floor. Screams and shouts of surprise echoed through the store.

When the tremors stilled for a moment, he hurried to the front. The clerk in the checkout lane did her best—totaling up the aerosol cans, taking his money, putting his purchases in a bag.

A voice came over the PA: "Everyone outside please."

Masami went for the exit. In the parking lot, waves rippled through the ground. Above, power lines coiled like snakes. The shaking wasn't vertical or horizontal but came from all directions at once. Tiles slid off the roof of a house as another swell surged—as if a giant below the earth was tossing in its sleep.

Before he could see or hear it, he felt the convulsions fading through the soles of his feet. Around him, the other customers who'd been in the store were checking their cell phones, and his hand went for his pocket as well. When his screen blinked on, he saw he didn't have a signal. Among the crowd of people who'd run out of Cainz Home, there was one old man who took a portable AM-FM receiver out of his car and started tuning it. Gradually everyone in the lot drifted toward the radio's staticky crackle.

The man turned the dial, closing in on the voice of an announcer who was struggling to stay calm: "A large tsunami warning is being issued for coastal Fukushima Prefecture. Please leave coastal areas and evacuate to elevated ground. For the earthquake that occurred at 2:46 p.m., strong level-6 tremors are being reported in Shirakawa, Sukagawa, Nihonmatsu, Kagamiishi, Naraha, Tomioka, Okuma, Futaba, Namie, and Shinchi... at 3:10 p.m., the forecast is for a three-meter tsunami along the Fukushima coast. The forecast is for a three-meter tsunami. Please leave coastal areas. Please evacuate to elevated ground. Tsunami arrival predictions for Fukushima Prefecture: Iwaki City, Onahama, 3:30 p.m., three-meter waves; Souma City, 3:40 p.m., three-meter waves..."

It was almost three and the highway that led back to Namie ran along the coast. Masami's land was in the hills, out of danger from any waves, but he had no idea if the house or outbuildings were damaged. He couldn't even call Shizue, his sister who lived on the ranch with him. He had to get back. Until he did, time would be a vise squeezing the minutes together—compressing them out of existence.

He jumped in his truck, threw his shopping in the cab, and fired up the engine. He whipped out of the parking lot, steering for the highway.

The road had sunk and cracked in places, and traffic was already stacking up. In half an hour, a wall of water would crash over the shore and flood the road in three places. The land between the highway and the sea would be inundated, the houses there crushed and washed away. But Masami didn't know this. As he drove—the gray ocean only a couple kilometers away, a few whitecaps rolling across the otherwise peaceful water—he was thinking only of home.

Yoshizawa Ranch was almost eighty acres in rural Namie, the product of two generations of his family's efforts to wrench success out of failure, tragedy, and collapse. It had started with his father; his old man had gone to Manchuria during the Second World War as a government-sponsored farm-settler, and, following the war, had somehow survived three years in a Soviet prison camp; he'd returned to Yotsukaido, in Chiba Prefecture, where he started another farm and a family. Masami and his older brother and sister were born there in the Kanto region, near Tokyo, but when real estate grew expensive and the government began dividing the land into smaller parcels—to build freeways and an international airport in Narita— his father, who'd been hoping to buy a bigger plot, sold and moved up north to Namie, in Fukushima. He worked hard to establish a dairy; he was still working the day he was pinned beneath a tractor and killed at the age of sixty-five. Masami's older brother had taken over the operation, but it wasn't long before he became involved with a woman who promised him marriage if he gave her a little money and then a little more. By the time Masami intervened—suing his own brother to keep him from selling their family's acreage—all the heifers had been auctioned off. After his brother left for Kyushu, never to return, Masami wasn't sure what to do with the land that he'd fought so hard to keep.

Jun Murata, a rancher from nearby Nihonmatsu, had suggested Masami try beef instead of dairy cows. Jun had given Masami forty head and brought him into the M Ranch Company's operation. It had taken a decade, but by the time the earthquake struck Masami was responsible for 328 black cows. Jun had hired two veterinarians, a husband-and-wife team from Kyoto, who lived in a prefab house on the ranch in Namie and were responsible for breeding the cattle and looking after the animals' health. Eventually, Masami hoped to have a herd of six hundred.

To build the two barns where he sheltered his cows, he'd learned how to weld, pour concrete, and run wiring. He knew every imperfection of the cowsheds, every rusted bolt and loose gutter. The house would be fine, he told himself as he sped down the highway—it had been built with steel-reinforced concrete and had a woodstove for heat—it was the barns he worried about.

Fed up with the crawling pace of traffic, he turned off the highway and took the back roads. It was nearly an hour before he reached the ranch, and the dirt and sweat and shit smell of the cattle greeted him as he pulled in. The top of a small rise in the driveway gave him a view of the whole property; the cowsheds were still standing, though the quake had split the ground in the main pasture that occupied the bulk of the land, leaving gashes of fresh dirt in the valley's grassy floor. The power would be out, the electric fences down, though the cows hadn't realized this.

He didn't drive all the way to the house and, instead, parked next to a collection of trucks, tractors, and trailers on a patch of gravel behind the northernmost barn. The acreage formed a rough circle, and the driveway entered the property from the north, skirted the eastern boundary until it came to the southern edge, curved west with the property line, and ended at the house.

He climbed out of his truck and took in the damage. The small shed he'd built for the well pump beside the house had collapsed, and the outflow pipe that sent water from the ranch's elevated cistern to the cows' watering troughs was busted.

"Shit," he muttered.

He didn't see the two veterinarians who also lived on the ranch and figured his sister and her son would be home, though he didn't go inside. He needed to get the water flowing. The herd drank several thousand liters a day. Even more than hay or grain, his cows lived on water.

Without electricity, the main well's pump was offline, and anyway, fixing the piping would take time. He decided to try to get the house's pump running; it was close to the barn and he could reconnect it to the house once he'd watered the herd.

He kept a welding torch, oxygen tank, and generator in the back of a light truck just in case, so he hopped in the mud-crusted Mitsubishi and put it in gear. He backed the truck up the slight slope beside the house and killed the engine. Tossing aside splintered pieces of siding, he found the pump's electric line and plugged it into the generator, but when he got it running, the pressure was weak. Only a trickle came from the barn's spigots. It would take him hours to fill the troughs. By the time he'd finished the daylight had all but faded.

With the cows seen to, Masami went inside. His cell had no signal, but there was a landline in the house. He dialed Jun and told his boss about the damages to the ranch but said that with the water back on they were fine for the moment.

After hanging up, he asked Shizue for the keys to her car. "I want to watch the news."

With the power out he couldn't watch TV in the house, but he could tune into digital One-Seg channels on her Subaru's navigation system.

He went out to where her car was parked in front of the house, got in the driver's seat, and turned the key so that the car's paperback-sized dashboard monitor flickered on. On NHK, they were playing footage from Natori, Miyagi Prefecture, a suburb of Sendai about an hour's drive north. The video had been taken from the air and showed the tsunami: a black tide of broken boards, burning houses, and swept-up boats; a stain spreading across rice fields, blotting out a greenhouse and chasing a car down a road. The shot switched to a different video, starting a series of clips, though he didn't see any shots of Minami-Souma or Namie. He did notice the message scrolling across the bottom of the screen: *Those within a three-kilometer radius of the Fukushima Daiichi Power Plant are instructed to evacuate, those within ten kilometers are advised to stay indoors.*

If he stood on the porch and faced the ocean, he could see the plant's ventilation towers on the horizon. The power station's name ticking across the bottom of the screen was like a dark cloud he'd long feared appearing on the horizon.

When he first moved to Fukushima, TEPCO had already been operating the Daiichi plant in Okuma for six years. Another electric utility wanted to build a new nuclear power station a few kilometers up the coast, on a piece of land that straddled both Namie and Minami-Souma; locals were fighting the plan and Masami identified with them. Growing up in the 60s and 70s, he'd come of age during an era of mass demonstrations, as entire swaths of society challenged the country's postwar order. When he was a high school student in Chiba, the farmers around Narita had joined forces with New Left groups in Tokyo to fight the construction of an international airport on their land. The riot police's armored buses passed on the highway in front of his school, while trains packed with protestors from the universities rattled over the tracks behind the baseball field. Seeing the college kids alongside the farmers— the former with their glasses and flowing hair, the latter with their work boots and stained undershirts, but all of them wearing hardhats covered in hand-scrawled slogans and standing behind bamboo barricades—had opened his eyes to the possibility of resistance. Later, at Tokyo University of Agriculture, Masami was elected student body president and managed to catch the tail end of the demonstrations against the Vietnam War and the American military's use of the ports. Never an academic standout, his proudest moments came during the marches, when he got on the megaphone to denounce the government, the US-Japanese Security Treaty, or war in general.

After graduating and coming to work on his father's dairy, he'd taken a similar stance toward the nuclear power facilities in the area. Though he wasn't a member of any political party, he became familiar with the local leftists; a former Communist Party candidate gave him an enormous speaker, which he mounted on top of a little Honda van. When the government in Minami-Souma began building a garbage-burning facility, he drove out and used it to protest the toxic gases it would release.

He was the type to throw himself into projects, whether it be the ranch or a political protest. A forceful, somewhat impulsive man, he was always questioning. The night after the tsunami, he grew curious and decided to take a look at the damage for himself.

He told his sister he was going out and bumped down the driveway in her little Subaru Stella. The trees on either side of the country roads thinned as he approached Namie's center. There wasn't any power in the town either, and, without streetlights, the cluster of houses and shops was the same pitch color as the surrounding forest. The few sources of light stood out amid the preindustrial dark, and, as he drove, Masami drifted toward their glow. In front of the fire station, they'd put up a huge white tent and ringed it with floodlights; firefighters bustled between stacks of rescue equipment in their navy-blue uniforms. The police station and town office were also lit up and busy with armies of officials planning their counteroffensive to the tsunami.

In the glimpses of the town that he caught in the car's headlights, he saw cracked walls, broken flowerpots, fissures in the asphalt—but nothing so terrible as what he'd seen in the news.

By the time he got home, it was late. In the dark, the ranch was different; the cattle were quiet in their sheds, the pastures were fields of silence. It wasn't until he was in the house that he noticed the distant thudding. His sister and nephew would be up in their rooms, but Shizue had left a candle burning in the living room for him. He stood in front of the window, facing the ocean and the plant, looking past his own reflection for the source of the sound. He spotted a red dot hovering in the air above the coast: a helicopter.

The realization that whatever was wrong with the plant was serious twisted through him. Though he'd never believed the claims about the power station's safety, he'd also never conceived of what the danger would look and feel like. Unlike the havoc he'd seen on the news, it was right out there, just below that tiny, crimson point of light.

Beyond his vision, encased in reinforced-concrete buildings and the thick walls of containment vessels, rods of uranium oxide were submerged in water, glowing the same brilliant blue as the hottest part of the flame. In three of the reactors, the water level was dropping.

March 12

Like most ranchers, Masami was an early riser. The sun hadn't been up long, but he was already outside getting ready to feed. The nicotine from his morning cigarette and the crisp air were sweeping the last cobwebs of sleep from his mind when he saw the police.

Three blue vans pulled up the driveway, the lights on their roofs flashing red, sirens muted. He knew it had to do with the helicopter he'd seen above the nuclear plant and what he'd heard on the news. There was a problem. They would ask him to evacuate.

"I can't go," he would say. "I have my cows."

As he walked toward where the police officers had parked on his driveway and were now unloading from their vehicles, a middle-aged officer approached Masami.

"Hello," he said, bowing. "We're with the Fukushima Police Communications Division. We—we'd like to set up a relay antenna on a corner of your property, if you don't mind. Our helicopter is filming the plant." The ranch was elevated, clear of trees and tall buildings, and had sight lines all the way to the ocean. "We need to send the footage to the main office so they can monitor the situation."

In general, Masami distrusted authority, but, face-to-face with the officer, there wasn't any reason not to cooperate. The prefectural police were headquartered in Fukushima City, about seventy kilometers away, and a dozen or so men had piled out of the vans. More than anything, he was glad they weren't there to force him off his land.

"Yes, that's fine," he said.

The permission relieved the officer of his request, and, as he turned and went back to his colleagues, they were already unpacking equipment. They moved like a crew of roadies setting up for a concert; from the back of the vans, they produced a generator, a foldout table, and several rolls of cables that were plugged into a dish-shaped antenna, which they pointed toward the plant.

Around the same time Masami was talking to the officer, Prime Minister Naoto Kan was coming up from Tokyo in a Self-Defense Forces helicopter. At 7:11 a.m., Masami wouldn't notice the slight change in the sound of the rotor blades as the country's political leader flew over the stricken plant. Only later, when he heard about it on the news, would he realize how thoroughly the world's attention had been drawn to his corner of Tohoku.

But that morning, if he ignored the police, might've been any late-winter day. To feed, he used the claw attachment on his tractor to take one of the round three hundred-kilogram bales from a stack on a pad of asphalt next to the driveway and carry it to the nearest barn. With a shovel, he pushed the dried grass into the feed troughs on either side. The cattle jostled for position, and soon the barn was loud with their chewing and plaintive lows rising from the crowded pens. As he was feeding in the other barn, his sister came outside wrapped in a coat.

"What did they want?" she asked, glancing at the police.

He repeated the explanation the officer had given him.

"Something strange is happening at the plant."

Though he hid it well, he felt the same worry he'd heard in his sister's voice. Without power, information about the plant was hard to come by. Even when he managed to catch a glimpse of the One-Seg channels in his sister's car, the news reports were vague and contradictory. As a rancher, he was tied to the land. He couldn't simply flee. Murata certainly didn't expect him to abandon the ranch.

Rather than sit with this feeling, he decided to go take a look at the shore to see if he couldn't get a better look than he had the night before. In the two-ton Isuzu, he took Route 114, which cut through the center of Namie, heading for the town's Ukedo district.

Early that morning, the evacuation zone had been expanded to everyone living within ten kilometers of the plant. Fire patrol trucks had driven around announcing the news, and loudspeakers mounted on telephone and electric poles throughout Namie had relayed the same message. From the ranch, he'd heard the garbled orders echoing through the neighborhoods below. As he drove toward the coast, the roads were clogged with Self-Defense Forces troop transports, police cruisers, buses, and cars piled with belongings—the whole town packed into the backs of minivans and station wagons, crammed into trunks and backseats.

After he passed the small downtown, the traffic thinned. Before the tsunami, Ukedo had been about 350 houses collected around a fishing port, but when Masami arrived at the coast, he saw that the district had been decimated.

He could still pick out shapes that resembled houses among the field of debris. The convex, curving white keel of a fishing trawler lay propped against the local fishing cooperative building; a blue-hulled skiff had been thrown into the structure's second floor and lay upside down on a concrete balcony. Cars were scattered everywhere, their metal crumpled and wrinkled like clothes just out of a washing machine, and several tile-roofed homes had collapsed into the street. But no matter how recognizable the shapes, the waves had destroyed any difference between the piles of rubble. The twisted beams and rent sheet metal were the same as the overturned refrigerators; even the dead bodies buried among the wreckage were just so much more debris. To Masami, it seemed like the end of the world.

To the south, above a hilly elbow of the coast, he could see the ventilation stacks and transmission towers of the Fukushima Daiichi plant. The power lines stretched into the distance, eventually meeting up with the cables that ran above Masami's property, and led all the way down to Tokyo.

The towers were no longer sending electricity to the capital, a problem that TEPCO and the Kan administration were trying to deal with. In the hours since the prime minister's visit that morning, the situation in Unit One had gotten worse—the reactor was cut off from power, the tsunami had flooded the backup batteries, and now the water level inside the core was low enough to expose the nuclear fuel.

In Okuma, Fukushima Daiichi's superintendent, Masao Yoshida, was in the plant's emergency response center, just fourteen kilometers from Masami's ranch—closer to the situation than either the government officials or his corporate bosses. While fission had stopped in each reactor after the quake, the fuel was still incredibly hot. The rods in Unit One were melting, the zirconium alloy that coated the uranium was reacting with the water to produce dangerous amounts of hydrogen. The fuel needed to be cooled to keep it from decomposing further and dropping into the bottom of the reactor, where it could burn right through the steel core. But the hydrogen pressure in the vessel was so high even fire trucks couldn't pump water in. Both Naoto Kan and TEPCO had agreed on the need to vent the reactor, and the prime minister had demanded the venting take place when he flew up. But Masao was the one who had to carry out the procedure, and, with no electricity, the vents had to be opened manually. His workers would have to venture outside in radiation suits, go into the dark, cramped spaces of the buildings, and operate unfamiliar equipment by hand. It was going to take time.

As he drove, Masami was aware of none of this. The night before, in the hours after the tsunami, Kan's Cabinet Secretary had said, "There is no radiation leak, nor will there be a leak," and TEPCO itself had put out a couple of blandly reassuring press releases. But just that morning the evacuation zone had been expanded, and Masami was anxious. If there was a leak, what would happen to his cows?

Back at the ranch, Masami parked and went in the house. Early that morning, his nephew, Atsushi, had gone to work at one of the local dairy farms, but Shizue was still home. As soon as Masami opened the door, a whiff of miso and the smell of cooking hit him. He found his sister in the kitchen; on a portable gas burner she was simmering a big pot of *hoto* soup, and he watched as she stirred the steaming broth, thick with noodles, leeks, and thin slices of pork.

"For the policemen," she said, looking up at him. "It's cold out."

While he could be single-minded to the point of neglect, his sister was expansive in the care she paid to the people around her. In the days after the tsunami, she showed just this quality. Once the food was ready, he helped her carry the meal outside. He took chopsticks, a ladle, and a stack of bowls, and she brought the big pot.

The men were surprised, and the lead officer accepted the pot, thanking Masami and his sister. "It looks delicious."

With this done, Masami turned back to his ranch. He had to run the generator for most of the day to make sure the cattle had enough water. He wasn't sure what he'd do if he ran out of fuel, but, for the moment, he was making do. As the afternoon grew late and cold, he thought to make sure the police were keeping warm.

For the past few years he'd been fashioning woodstoves out of empty gas cylinders by cutting off the ends, welding them together, opening a hole for a chimney, and attaching iron feet; he had a notion to try selling them—ranchers and folks who worked outside in a place as cold as Namie would appreciate the chance to warm up without having to drop everything and go in. He muscled one of these stoves into the bucket of a front-end loader and drove over to where the police vans were.

He caught the eye of the officer he'd spoken to before, saying, "You'll be cold, out here since the morning. You going to be here a couple more days?"

"Headquarters has just ordered us to withdraw—finally. Sorry, we have to go."

Dumbfounded, Masami stood watching the communication officers pack up the generator, the cables and antenna, their desk, and load them back in the vans. The cop whom he'd talked to thanked him again before getting in one of the vehicles. The lights on the roofs of the three vans were flashing red as they crept down the driveway and disappeared just as quickly as they'd arrived.

Occupied with his work, Masami hadn't heard the explosion—hadn't felt the ground move as the Unit One reactor at Fukushima Daiichi went up in a plume of white smoke. Later, he'd see it on TV. Footage from an NHK camera showed the muted blast; the plume seemed like that from a smoke bomb lit next to a model of the building. But when he saw a close up of the plant—the steel frame still intact but the concrete walls smashed out like the glass from a car window—he understood that whatever the structure had been containing was now in the air all around him.

At the plant, Superintendent Masao had mistaken the blast for another earthquake. Only when he saw the TV broadcast did he realize there'd been an explosion, though he didn't understand what had caused it. In the moment, Masao's staff didn't stop to debate the reason behind the detonation, and, instead, everyone turned their attention to the Unit Two and Three reactors, where water levels were low. The explosion had damaged the cables his employees had been laying to restore power to units one and two and the hoses they'd been preparing to pump seawater through. TEPCO was calling what had happened in Unit One—what was now going on in units two and three—"fuel pellet melt," avoiding the word meltdown, though that's exactly what it was.

At the ranch, the cops' departure had unsettled Masami. Though he'd heard there'd been an explosion, he didn't know what that meant for him, and he decided to see what the farmers at the local dairy collective were thinking. Yoshizawa Ranch had been a dairy for years, and he knew many of the members. Though their building was just five minutes up the road from the ranch, his nephew had said the power was back on there.

When he arrived, several vehicles were parked in the collective's gravel lot. He stopped his truck by the main building and found a handful of farmers gathered around a television in the meeting room.

"What are we going to do?" one of the men was asking.

Another answered, "This place is done for."

Without power, the dairymen couldn't milk their heifers, and if nothing changed, their cows would dry up. With the crisis at the plant compounding each hour, those who were making do with gas generators still faced customers afraid to buy milk from the area. They might as well toss their production.

Masami listened to the farmers and took the opportunity to charge his cell phone; he'd heard from his nephew that service had been restored. Then, a few minutes before 6:30 p.m., Naoto Kan appeared on the TV. As the prime minister walked to a podium, a map of the tsunami damage flashed red, yellow, and green in the corner of the screen. He wore a blue jumpsuit instead of his standard suit and tie and spoke slowly as, off camera, shutters continually clicked like cicadas.

"...We are putting the safety of local people first and taking the appropriate precautions. With regards to the Unit One reactor at Fukushima Daiichi, I've been listening to the latest update from my cabinet secretary and, because of present circumstances, following the evacuation of residents within ten kilometers of the plant, I am now ordering the evacuation of residents within twenty kilometers of Fukushima Daiichi."

Even as he heard the words, Masami knew he wouldn't flee. The extended zone fell over his ranch—his cattle, his land, the house—all of it lay within the red semicircle being drawn on maps the world over. It was worse than he'd ever imagined, and yet he would stay. He would outlast this.

March 14

The thought of his cows' empty stomachs was what got Masami moving in the small hours. Even when his body was stiff, it got him out of bed, and the same was true that morning.

The day before, he'd gone to see Murata at the M Ranch Company's main office in Nihonmatsu. Masami had no plans to leave, but the cattle didn't belong to him alone, and they needed to talk over what was to be done with the herd. The husband-and-wife veterinarian team had already fled to Kyoto with their children.

As things stood, there weren't a lot of options. They could try to ship the beef cows to one of M Ranch's customers, and Jun could distribute the younger heifers among his ranches outside the evacuation zone. But the mature cattle hadn't been slated for sale for a few months and were still lean from the winter. Moving them was a big operation, and that was if they could find anyone willing to buy cows from the evacuated area in the first place. Murata was dealing with these decisions in several iterations: out of the ranches in his company, four were within the evacuation zone; of the M Ranch's 1,200 or so cows, more than a third were on these properties.

With each animal liable to ask as much as a new car at market, he had a small fortune of stock at risk.

"We'll figure out something eventually," Murata had said.

On Monday, in the early light, Masami started up the generator that powered the well pump and was relieved to find none of the pipes had frozen. A cold front had moved in overnight, and it felt as though it might snow.

In the winter, long icicles grew from the edges of the barn roofs, and the stream running through the grazing pasture iced over. By March, all that remained were a few patches of dead gray frost hidden in the forest, though Namie was still in for a few deep chills. With the woodstove in the living room, Shizue, Atsushi, and he were plenty warm, though it'd been days since they'd had hot showers.

The same was true for Superintendent Yoshida, who was still at his post in the emergency response center at Fukushima Daiichi. His workers were strung out from sleeping in hallways and conference rooms with a single blanket each, wearing the same clothes for days, rationing water, and eating only two meals a day: crackers and boxes of vegetable juice in the morning, rice and curry or canned food at night. In the smoking room, Masao passed out cigarettes to support his team.

After the explosion of Unit One, their attention had turned to reactors two and three. Though they'd hooked a fire engine to Unit Three and were pumping seawater into the core, the instruments in the control room didn't show the water level rising. The day before, they'd vented the containment three times, and they tried again that morning, but the pressure kept climbing. On top of this, while reactor four had been offline for maintenance when the tsunami hit, the temperature was now rising in its spent fuel pool, the tank that stored used uranium rods as they cooled. The fuel under the water in the Unit Four building had been removed from the reactor months before, but it was still incredibly hot. If the water boiled off the fuel would be exposed. Masao needed to find a way to get water into that pool.

At 11:00 a.m., on the ranch, Masami was in his cowshed finishing the morning feed. The scrape of a shovel on concrete, the cows chewing hay, the slurp of their long gray tongues on the salt blocks—and then—all sound shattered by a clap of thunder, like a firework detonating far above the barn.

He knew where the sound had come from and hustled over to the house. A pillar of smoke was rising from the plant. His phone buzzed in his pocket. When he answered, it was Murata.

"There was just an explosion."

"I know. I heard it," Masami said. "What are we going to do?"

But there was no answer to his question. He almost thought he could feel the radiation washing over him, and, of course, his cattle were being bathed in the same particles.

At the plant, Masao Yoshida was scrambling—he didn't even understand what'd happened. The Self-Defense Forces' Nuclear Biological Chemical Weapon Unit had just driven onto the grounds when the blast ripped through the plant—gray dust surrounded the soldiers like a fog as they tried to gain their bearings, chunks of concrete showered down on them, and four of the men retreated, limping and clutching their injuries. The fire engine Masao's team had been using to pump seawater into the reactor was damaged and several TEPCO employees were hurt. The Unit Three building was a smashed, smoking skeletal ruin. Unlike Unit One, the upper half of the structure had collapsed in. The blast had been felt as far as forty kilometers away.

At his ranch, Masami watched the blast cloud floating up, the gray smoke trailing beneath, the plume moving across the sky like a jellyfish—seemingly slow, and yet fast for something of its size. He began to realize that this wouldn't be a temporary evacuation, there were no stopgap measures that could save his herd, and the hope that had held his world together faded with the same sickening speed as the haze of the explosion.

March 17

There was no food left in the house. He had used up his diesel running the generator, and, without fuel, he couldn't pump water for his cows. The gas stations nearby were all closed. His sister and nephew had fled two days before. He drove them to Murata's house, where the three of them spent the night. After talking over their options, they decided Shizue and Atsushi would drive down to join her husband in Chiba while Masami stayed behind. This was his home after all, and there wasn't room for him at his sister's house anyway. Now, he was truly alone.

He'd returned a day ago. After entering Namie, he ran into a police checkpoint on Highway 114, the road back to his ranch. The police had blocked the inbound lane with a blue van, and an electronic message on the roof read, *Entry Prohibited*. The cops were waving cars through the outbound lane, but when he pulled up, the officers motioned him to a stop with their orange and white traffic batons.

He rolled down his window as a man in a blue uniform and white helmet came around the front. The cop was young and polite, and after Masami explained that his ranch lay a few kilometers down the road, the boy calmly said, "I can see you're trying to get through, but I have to stop you. The lives of your cattle are important, but you also have to consider human life."

"I'll take responsibility for myself," Masami said. "If I leave them, they'll die."

After a moment's hesitation, the police officer waved him through.

He eased the truck back into gear and rolled into Tsushima. Passing through the district, he saw Self-Defense Force tents and clutches of refugees huddled around fires. It was like the scene behind a war front.

He saw cars turning in to the middle school, and he could imagine the overflowing parking lot, the crowded gym, the rectangles of cardboard on the basketball court heaped with winter blankets, shoes in the aisles. On TV, he'd seen the miserable evacuees had nothing but what they'd been able to grab from their homes as they fled, and now could count on only a bowl of rice from the authorities each morning. The temperatures were still dipping down near freezing at night, and the walls in those old school buildings were thin. Shizue had been against evacuating to Tsushima. She'd kept saying, "I just don't want wind up in one of those gyms."

After arriving at the ranch, he fed and watered the herd. He kept hearing explosions echoing out of the plant. There were reports that TEPCO might pull its people out, and the Kan administration was getting more involved by the hour. On top of all this, earlier in the day, Murata had called with bad news.

"They refused to take delivery." The buyer they'd been hoping would take the cattle had decided against it. "It's all over now."

"That's it then."

Later, from the second floor of the house, through an old pair of binoculars, he watched a twin-rotor helicopter circling the plant. They were bailing water from the ocean in enormous buckets and dumping it over the reactor buildings, trying to replenish the spent fuel pool in Unit Four, but the wind caught most of the water, turning it into curtains of mist that blew away from the building.

In their dedication, the Self-Defense Forces reminded Masami of the kamikaze pilots who'd sacrificed themselves for the country during the War. The TEPCO engineers might abandon their posts, but the Self-Defense Forces wouldn't flee. They would all die there. He was sure of it.

Still, no matter what the troops did they couldn't save his animals, and even if he kept his cows alive no one would buy them. It had been nearly a week since the disaster started, though he had no idea what he or his cattle had been exposed to. The government had a system called SPEEDI that assessed the spread of radioactive releases, but the system relied on the plant's measuring equipment, which was still offline. If SPEEDI couldn't predict how much radiation was being released, then it could at least calculate what direction the plume was moving. But claiming that the partial reports would only cause confusion, the government hadn't released them, and, so, the evacuees from Namie who'd gone to Tsushima didn't know they were fleeing into the worst of the radiation. Like Masami, they could only guess at the winds and the ions in the air. The land he'd fought for, had toiled so hard to make a profit on, was now just eighty acres from the disaster zone.

There was nothing left for him there.

That afternoon, for the first time, it dawned on him that he would leave, that he might never see the ranch again. He decided he would go to TEPCO's headquarters. He'd seen the building on TV: a dull, gray box in downtown Tokyo with an enormous orange antenna jutting out of it. He'd take the speaker car and find someone, make them listen.

There wasn't enough gas in the van's tank, so he went around the ranch siphoning fuel from the other vehicles into a washbasin and funneled it into the Honda. Before he left, he took the spray paint he'd bought on the day of the earthquake and, in giant letters, big enough for the Self-Defense Forces to see from the air, on the waste silo and the bucket of his biggest tractor he wrote: "Unite to save lives or die trying!"

In the coming years, as he became more involved in the anti-nuclear movement—hauling his radiated cows down to Tokyo and around the prefectural capitals; demanding compensation and that his animals be studied; giving speeches and leading marches of leftists; continuing to live on the ranch even when the government barricaded the roads and caught him sneaking onto his ranch and tried to make him promise not to return; and watching his neighbors' animals starve to death until their hides were scattered across the land like deflated leather balloons—he would hold the memory of the days after the quake to himself, a precious, inexhaustible energy that burned inside him.

But as he flew down the Tohoku Expressway his future was still cloudy. He knew nothing of what was to come. He drove toward Kanto and his heart beat like the flashing lights of the hundreds of police cars, fire trucks, and Self-Defense Force vehicles that passed him, heading the other direction.

Refuge

March-April 2011

I. All the Suits in Tokyo

Chiyoda Ward, Tokyo

Masami arrived at the Tokyo Electric Power Company's headquarters near midnight. He'd been on the highway most of the night, driving four hours south on Route 4.

The electric utility's building was next to the Shinbashi nightlife district, but, that Thursday, instead of office workers getting an early start on the weekend, the streets were crowded with television news vans and police cars. Aside from the media and the cops, the streets outside the company's headquarters were empty. The bars lining the narrow alleys were dark.

Before leaving Fukushima, Masami had gone to see the head of the M Ranch Company, which owned the cattle that Masami had tended to on his land. He told Murata he was going to Tokyo, and his boss said, in that case, Masami would be their representative in the city.

Masami asked if his boss would file suit for compensation, and Murata said, "Of course."

"Let's pluck it off them," Masami agreed.

Now, seeing the massive building in the middle of the capital, its lights blinking in the night, he shook with anger. First thing in the morning, he would demand to speak with someone from the utility. He had to. After all, the dairy workers in Namie, whose farms neighbored his ranch, weren't the type to complain or speak out. Everyone was looking after their own: their families, their animals, their land. He'd done the same, but, in the end, there had been no saving his cattle. With him gone, all 328 cows on his ranch would starve or die of thirst. There was no helping it.

What he could do was to make sure the suits in charge of TEPCO took notice. Of course, they'd claim the tsunami had been unforeseeable; it was a natural disaster and they weren't to blame.

But, in the face of so much destruction, everyone was doing their duty—police officers and firefighters were scouring the tsunami debris for survivors; Self-Defense Forces pilots were flying their helicopters right at the radioactive reactors, while, inside the plant, the skeleton crew led by Masao Yoshida was working through the night to bring the disaster under control.

Everyone was making sacrifices. Everyone, save for the TEPCO executives, sitting in their office tower, far from the danger they'd created. After returning from a business trip in Osaka, the president and CEO of the company, Masataka Shimizu, had put on a blue worker's uniform, given a dry press conference, and then had promptly disappeared from public view. Shimizu hadn't turned up to testify with the head of the Nuclear and Industrial Safety Agency before Parliament, and the doorman at his upscale apartment building, The Tower, hadn't seen him. Rumor was, he'd fled or committed suicide.

For years, even as the company had told the public how safe nuclear power was, its leaders had ignored regulators' demands for higher seawalls at Fukushima Daiichi and improvements to the reactor's emergency systems. Meanwhile, the turbines at the plant had generated untold profits, sending electricity straight to Tokyo on the high-voltage power lines that crossed Masami's land. The power produced at the plant hadn't brightened so much as a light bulb for people in Namie.

Negligence, not the tsunami, had led to a man-made disaster. So, while Masami wasn't sure what it would accomplish, he planned to ask for an interview loud enough and long enough that they wouldn't be able to ignore him.

But it was still the middle of the night. He would have to wait until the morning. He pulled his van onto a side street, parked, and got as comfortable as he could in the little Honda, though he knew he wouldn't be able to sleep.

March 18

Masami started the day with a visit to the cops. The Marunouchi Police Station was a tan high-rise a couple blocks from the TEPCO building and across the street from the brown-green water that ringed the grounds of the Imperial Palace.

Inside the station house, the low ceilings and fluorescent lighting gave the space a worn, institutional feel, but the heating was a reprieve from the cold night Masami had spent in the van. He found the appropriate desk and asked for permission to use his speaker car; it was a few minutes before the officer came back with a polite but flat refusal. It was too early, the cop said. Masami needed to wait until after eight thirty in the morning.

But he was through waiting. He wasn't the type to hold things in; he was used to speaking his mind, doing as he saw fit. What had happened to his ranch, his cows—was all stuck inside him.

Back in his van, he put on his M Ranch jacket and baseball cap, made sure he had his business cards, and set out for the utility on foot. He rounded a corner and saw the TEPCO building, its enormous red-and-white antenna jutting out of the roof. He walked right at the police barricade in front of the tower. Already, an officer in a navy shirt and white gloves was moving toward him.

"I'm a rancher from the town of Namie in Fukushima," he said, as five or six cops closed in on him. "Because of them I can't water my cattle.

Because of them I don't have feed. My cows are dying. That's why I'm here."

The officers seized his arms. His outburst had set the police buzzing, and they pressed in around him.

He went to speak, but his voice snapped in his throat. A guttural wail roared out of him, his face was wet, and he felt everything pouring out. His bawling surprised the cops, and they seemed to hear him for the first time, as he repeated himself in broken fragments. Between the officers' shoulders and through his tears, he made out the automatic doors of the entrance. They were only a few meters away, but they might as well have been on the other side of a moat. The police talked among themselves, and, eventually, an officer contacted the staff of the TEPCO building.

The morning was cold—overnight it had dipped down near freezing—but Masami didn't feel a thing. For several minutes, he stood wiping his eyes while the cops bunched around him, and then the front entrance's doors opened.

One of the police told him to go ahead. "They'll hear you out."

He walked up to the front entrance. A secretary was waiting on the other side of the doors, and Masami walked into the lobby. Rich wood paneling covered the walls, save for a section of white behind the reception desk where the utility's name was spelled out in orange stylized letters like a video game logo. The representative took him to a large meeting room adjacent to the lobby, with a coffee table and several plush sofas, and told him to sit.

After a few minutes, two plainclothes officers came into the room, introduced themselves, and were then followed by a man in a suit. This executive gave a stiff, silent bow to Masami and held out his card. Masami returned the greeting and exchanged business cards with the company's representative, before lowering himself onto the couch. The man sat on the sofa facing him, and the two cops took their places on either side of him as if they were afraid Masami was going to try to jump the guy right there.

Masami had distilled all he wanted to say down to two points, and he prepared to deliver them as he fingered the stiff piece of paper the executive had handed him. It said this man worked in the General Affairs Group.

Masami's first point was simple enough: he repeated what he'd said about his herd of 328 cows, which he'd gradually grown over the last ten years, and which was now entirely worthless and dying of thirst and hunger on his ranch that very moment. His company would sue for compensation. The representative accepted the half-warning, half-request as a matter of course. By then, everyone with access to a working television knew the company would soon be dealing with hundreds, if not thousands, of lawsuits and would be paying compensation for years to come. There was already speculation that the utility would have to be nationalized, as there was no way it could meet these obligations on its own.

Masami's second point was more personal, and he looked the man full in the face as he started in: "How could you have pulled men away from the plant? How could you? When the Self-Defense Forces and police are doing the most dangerous work? Why can't you take responsibility for the reactors you built, the reactions you started? Now, the important thing is to be prepared to die. If it were me, I'd think nothing of giving my life. I'd jump into the reactor with a fire hose if I had to. You should be willing to put your own life on the line."

Half-weeping, he flung the thoughts that he'd had no one to tell at the man for nearly a half hour. By the time he was finished, the general affairs executive was crying as well.

As Masami got up, left the meeting room, walked out of the lobby, and through the police barricade, a sense of satisfaction rose up within him. Coming down here had meant something. If he'd been able to express just a fraction of the anger and devastation he felt to the utility, then it hadn't been in vain.

Encouraged, he returned to the Marunouchi Police Station and asked again for permission to use the speakers on his Honda. He wanted to drive around the center of Tokyo and tell people what the media and politicians weren't saying. He submitted his request, and four officers came to him with the answer. It turned out one of these men was the station chief, and his refusal was more to the point: "It's important what you're doing, it's great, but you have to understand, so many people were washed away by the tsunami, so many are still missing. It's too early. We can't give you permission today."

Later, Masami would see the sense in this. In Tokyo, there had been food and water shortages, blackouts in some areas. On the day of the quake, with the Shinkansen and other train lines suspended, some commuters had walked for hours to get home. The shock of the disaster was still fresh in the city.

Unable to broadcast his message, Masami decided to make a few house calls instead. One was to the Nuclear and Industrial Safety Agency, NISA, the government body in charge of regulating nuclear plants. In addition to being a watchdog, NISA was also tasked with promoting the nuclear industry—a clear conflict of interest. As with so many of the institutions and leaders involved with nuclear power—the politicians, who promoted it as stable, clean energy, which would help them fight global warming; the local leaders, who sold it as a source of jobs for their shrinking towns;

the construction companies with political ties, which could make billions building the plants and the infrastructure around them; the electric utilities, which had government guarantees to sell the nuclear power they generated for high prices—there were few incentives for scrutiny and caution. Indeed, in the months ahead, as outside analysts and legislative panels picked through the bombed-out rubble of the Fukushima Daiichi plant, NISA would come under serious criticism. A year after the disaster, the agency would be abolished.

After telling off the bureaucrats at NISA, Masami dropped in on the offices of Yukio Edano, Chief Cabinet Secretary to Prime Minister Kan. Masami had seen Edano on TV, saying there would be "no significant release of radiation," using the expression "explosion-like event," and doing everything he could to avoid saying meltdown. What had happened at the plant weren't explosion-like events. They were explosions. Why couldn't he say it? But when Masami showed up in Edano's office and explained that he wanted to see the cabinet secretary, a staffer told him he needed an appointment. A couple of cops showed up to escort Masami out of the building.

Another stop on his whirlwind tour was the Ministry of Agriculture. There, he begged the civil servants to help his animals. Wasn't there anything they could do? Of course, Masami had been raising his cows to sell them for slaughter, but his animals lived several good years before that: grazing in the green valley of the ranch by day, huddling together in the warm barns by night. Every year, several dozen were sold off, and even more were birthed. There was a balance. He'd helped birth the cows in his herd now, pulling the breach calves from their mothers' wombs and feeding them by bottle if they couldn't nurse. To lose them all at once was to lose a part of himself.

Afraid that, with the electric fences down, his animals would get out and damage his neighbors' property, he'd left them in the barns—the gates closed. There was no one to feed or fill their troughs. He'd been gone a day; soon they would begin to collapse, their heads still in between the metal bars of the feed troughs, waiting to be fed.

Even as Masami drove his Honda van between the headquarters of the various bureaucracies in Tokyo, what he didn't know was that, on that day he'd left, Jun Murata had made a trip out to Yoshizawa Ranch.

Looking at one of the sheds, packed with animals steaming in the cold, he felt bitter about everything that had happened. The animals had lost all their value, but, if allowed to roam free, they'd likely bust through the fences and cause havoc to the farm and neighboring properties. Still, knowing this was little comfort in light of the fact that, in a few days, the whole herd would starve to death. Overcome with emotion, he went to the metal fence at the end of the barn and pulled out the pin that held the gate closed.

The black cows flowed out of the shed and into the irradiated pastureland, where shoots of green grass were sprouting on the valley floor.

II. Into the Mountains

Koriyama City, Fukushima Prefecture

Four days after the quake and three days after leaving Okuma, Katsue Sakai decided to go back. Everywhere within twenty kilometers of the plant was under mandatory evacuation orders, which meant if the police caught her, she'd be arrested. Still, she had to go.

At Northern Koriyama Industrial High School, Tsuneo and she had food and shelter, though only she slept in the gymnasium, while Tsuneo spent his nights in the car with their cat Coo. However, she'd left most of her money and valuables in her apartment, and it didn't feel good to be so dependent. If they wanted anything—blankets to keep them warm in the car overnight or wet food for Coo—they couldn't just go and buy it like before.

She also fretted over what was happening in her hometown. There were reports of thieves wandering evacuated areas and robbing the empty houses. Mixed in with these rumors were whispers from the other refugees of secret trips back to Okuma. The police and the Self-Defense Forces were busy. No one was watching the highway.

"We went home," a friend told her. "Just to get our valuables."

Every day, the news was about the accidents at the nuclear plant. After the reactor explosions, the television commentators started worrying about spent fuel pools—massive water-filled tanks where the uranium rods were stored after being used—it took decades for the rods to cool down, and if new water wasn't pumped in, the water might boil off, exposing the fuel, until it grew hot enough to burn through the building and into the earth itself.

Though the government hadn't expanded the evacuation zone, the US Embassy was telling its citizens not to go within eighty kilometers of the plant. For Katsue and Tsuneo, there was no telling when they'd be able to go back, and there was no one at the shelter Katsue could ask to find out. Would it be a week? A month?

She just wanted to go and grab a few things. They'd been ordered to leave, but, according to the rumors, there weren't any checkpoints to stop them from going. They talked about radiation, but how much harm could it do her? No one had gotten sick yet.

"If everyone's sneaking back home, let's go," she said to Tsuneo.

They left early, in the quiet of the morning. They drove out of the city, Coo in her carrier in her usual spot in the backseat.

Koriyama lay in a valley that ran north to south between two mountain ranges, and the traffic thinned as their Honda climbed the road that ran up into the eastern hills, separating the city from the coast. Soon, the forest moved in on either side of the road, and the houses disappeared. They watched for patrol cars or Self-Defense Force vehicles, but the rumors had been right. There was no one.

It was an hour and a half to Okuma, and afternoon was coming on by the time they drove out of the hills and down into the ghost of their town. Everything was just as it had been right after the earthquake: roof tiles fallen in a heap in the street, bicycles leaning on their kickstands by the train station, curtains of a shop window pulled open so the plants inside could still get daylight, the main road impassable where the shaking had ripped cracks in the asphalt. It was if the town was waiting for the residents to return and start fixing it up.

From afar, the small cluster of houses and stores had seemed still, but as Tsuneo turned through the streets, they saw cats and dogs that had been left behind in the evacuation. These pets trotted across the road as if they'd never known anything but freedom, but they weren't wild animals. Most would starve within days.

Katsue and Tsuneo didn't let themselves get sidetracked and headed straight to the public housing block where they'd lived for so many years. In the parking lot, she listened to the quiet, knowing she found it eerie only because of what it signified. She put the feeling aside and followed Tsuneo up the stairs to the third floor.

At first, her only thought had been to get their valuables and the little cash they had stashed away in their apartment. Though once they were in their rooms, which were still littered with things that'd fallen during the quake, she realized it might be a long time before they'd be back. Even more than her parent's house—a half-collapsed wooden building on a plot of land by the Kuma River where she'd been raised—she'd thought of the apartment as home. But, before long, the rooms would just be an abandoned space in an empty building.

They moved quick, speaking little, always with the thought in the back of their minds that they needed to get back before they were found out, or before someone at the gym noticed they were gone. She grabbed her Toho Bank account book, a few of Coo's playthings, and helped Tsuneo fold up a thick comforter and the blanket from the *kotatsu* table so that he wouldn't be so cold sleeping in the car.

Back in the Honda, she took one last look at the deserted parking lot before Tsuneo pulled onto the road, heading west.

March 18

In the days after their trip to Okuma, time stretched out for Katsue and Tsuneo. The Sakais had worked all their lives and weren't used to being idle. The refugee shelter was better than nothing, but it was also only a step from homelessness. Each person or family had claimed a space on the hardwood floor and filled it with a sleeping pad, indoor slippers, and other supplies provided by the Self-Defense Forces. There were no walls. The best they could do was put up low barriers of cardboard around their spaces for a little bit of privacy.

Nights in the car, Tsuneo covered himself with one of the blankets from the apartment. At mealtimes, Katsue and Tsuneo chatted with each other as they picked at the rice and soup with their chopsticks. The high school's alumni, the city's hospital cooperative association, and other local groups brought loads of tinned meat, canned tuna and mackerel, fresh apples, and the sweet winter oranges Koriyama was known for. Local volunteers would come to cook simple but delicious one-pot meals of curry and pork soup.

But the food was small comfort. The network of friends and acquaintances Katsue would normally have relied on to figure out what was going on was now dispersed all over the prefecture, all over the country. A few days after arriving at the shelter, Masako Iida had been able to get in touch with her nephew, and she and her husband had left to stay with him.

Katsue got in touch with her own daughter a week after the disaster. Like Katsue, after college her daughter had found a job in Kanto, the region around Tokyo. While working at Panasonic, she'd met a man, gotten married, and now lived with him in Saitama Prefecture. Over the phone, she asked, "Mama, where are you?"

Katsue said, "Because of the way everything happened we wound up at a high school in Koriyama."

There was no use in her daughter coming to visit them in the gymnasium, and Katsue and Tsuneo weren't about to drive down and impose themselves on her. Besides, they'd already spent too much time on the road. The travel wore on Coo, whose fur was getting patchy in places.

But Katsue was beginning to realize they might be living like this for a while. Each day brought some new crisis at the nuclear plant and, while she'd had faith in the town hall before the disaster, now it was clear the authorities were just as lost, just as bumbling, as the refugees themselves had been during the evacuation—as they'd run first here and then there like deer flushed from a forest.

In the days after the first meltdown, Okuma's administration had been all but liquidated. The mayor and his staff had been getting incomplete information, which was outdated by the time the town hall relayed it to the residents. As a result, decisions about where to send refugees had been ad hoc: people were sent anywhere there was space; food was handed out as it arrived.

But, while Katsue and Tsuneo were living in the refugee shelter, the response was starting to become more organized. Having been mobilized by the federal government, the Self-Defense Forces established ration supply routes, and began clearing the roads and conducting search and rescue operations. Slowly, Okuma's mayor was starting to coordinate with the prefectural government to find more permanent shelter for the roughly 7,500 residents of the town who were still in Fukushima. The town's superintendent of schools had advised him that families with children were eager to get their kids settled before the academic year started at the beginning of April. The mayor was preparing to make a request for where he wanted the town's residents relocated, and the prefectural Disaster Response Center would review this ask to make sure the area he'd selected could accommodate that many people.

Once the local and prefectural government had agreed on a place to send the residents of Okuma, work could begin on building temporary housing units. The Ministry of Land, Infrastructure, Transport, and Tourism, one of the sprawling federal bureaucracies in Tokyo, was tasked with this feat of construction. Until these units were finished, residents would live in public facilities, hotels, and even traditional *ryokans*, with the town paying their room and board.

The gears of this process kept grinding on, and an official from Okuma town eventually came to the shelters, offering up sixty-thousand yen in emergency, no-interest loans to the refugees.

Of course, Katsue and Tsuneo took the money. But what Katsue really wanted was to know when they'd be allowed back. She knew it wouldn't be right away, but if they would just tell her she'd be going home in three, or even six, months that would have put her at ease. But it had been a week since the disaster, and still they heard nothing.

April 7
More than three weeks after arriving at Northern Koriyama Industrial High School, Katsue helped Tsuneo pack their few possessions into the back of the Honda. They were moving on to their second shelter. Despite the weeks they'd spent in the gymnasium, it took only a couple trips from the school to the chilly parking lot to get everything. As they began driving inland, Tsuneo was behind the wheel and Coo was in her carrier in the backseat.

Two weeks before, they'd been told they were moving. By the time the mayor came with a group of staff from the town hall, Katsue had been sleeping and living at the high school for so long, with no idea of what would come next, that the days had begun to bleed into one another. Mayor Watanabe usually wore a tie and a three-piece pinstriped suit, but that day he turned up in a gray worker's uniform. He had square glasses that accentuated the shape of his blocky face. The official announcement had been made the day before, but, as Katsue listened, he explained that the bulk of Okuma Town's residents would move to Aizu-Wakamatsu, a city deep in the mountains.

The remaining residents would be dispersed across the prefecture, with most of the rest going to Iwaki. Residents could submit requests for the type of housing they wanted: handicap accessible, near a school, close to a hospital, and so on. After submitting their requests, Katsue and Tsuneo were assigned to the Nekoma Hotel in Ura-Bandai. She had never been to the area, but she knew it was near Mount Bandai, the famous peak near the huge lake at the heart of the prefecture. Out there, she'd be closer to the Sea of Japan than to her hometown on the Pacific coast.

What choice did they have? Thus, almost a month after evacuating, she and Tsuneo found themselves on the road again. As they drove up into the mountains, the patches of snow in the ditches and forests beside the road grew wider, spreading and connecting up with one another. That and the piles of firewood stacked in front of the houses were markers of the harsh inland winters.

They came around a turn, and there was the mountain. It was covered in a sheet of snow that looked hard as glass; past the lower peaks, the pinnacle of the mountain thrust toward the clouds like a ladder made of rock.

Pulling off the Ban-etsu Expressway, they followed a road that skirted the base of the mountain. They passed log homes, upscale restaurants, and cafés that stood out among the rusting metal siding of the farmhouses. It wasn't until they pulled into the main part of Ura-Bandai that the log-cabin-style buildings took over, the hotels and coffee shops leading toward the ski lifts like a trail of breadcrumbs. But the ski season was over. Most stores were closed.

At last, the sign for the Nekoma Hotel's parking lot appeared. The hotel's three enormous wings, each several stories high, were connected end to end at obtuse angles that ran parallel to the shore of the lake on the other side of the hotel. Although the tall arches of the entrance and the dormer windows jutting out of the roof gestured toward a kind of tourist attraction, it also gave off a bit of the feel of a concrete fortress. The hotel had been built at the very end of the postwar economic bubble, when elaborate resorts and amusement parks had sprung up all over the country. It had a café, a bar, an *onsen*, and rooms for several hundred guests.

Tsuneo found a spot in the lot and turned off the Honda's engine. Even as Katsue stepped out of the car and helped him gather their things, she wondered what kind of life awaited them there. Sitting around drinking canned coffee with the other survivors every afternoon? Talking just to talk? Bathing at night and looking out on at the lake from the steaming outdoor pool? Afternoons she would venture into the snowy landscape, the mountains towering over her on all sides.

Then, as now, there would be nothing she could do about her and Tsuneo's lot. She would simply pull her coat tighter around herself and try to move on.

III. The Barber of Kamaishi Elementary

Kamaishi City, Iwate Prefecture
The night after the disaster, Keitaro couldn't sleep.

Along with the half-dozen JA Bank employees, the six survivors from the city bus, and his neighbor, he'd made his way through the wreckage to the elementary school. When they arrived, the school was already swarmed with survivors. After the tsunami, over seven hundred people sought shelter in Kamaishi Elementary, one of the city's designated evacuation areas.

The Owatari Neighborhood Association's storage shed was next to the school, and, as soon as the waves crested, the local disaster response volunteers had gathered to ready the emergency supplies—fueling the generators and preparing to disperse water and blankets. The gym and all the classrooms were pressed into service as sleeping spaces, and, as refugees poured in, the volunteers asked for the refugees names, addresses, and ages, so they could write up a list of survivors.

Keitaro found himself packed into an unused classroom with three-dozen other survivors. In the dark, his own sense of shock wrapped around him like a haze. At some point, one of the neighborhood association volunteers handed each survivor a single rice cracker, which would be their dinner. He was also given a blanket and watched as the others spread their coverings on the floor in lieu of mattresses. But even though the day had been exhausting, Keitaro couldn't sleep. He couldn't help remembering the corpses he'd seen on the bus, as lifeless as all the other rubble.

All night, he sat on a chair, his blanket across his shoulders, replaying the events of the day in his mind. After the earthquake, his first thought had been to head for his familial home. But the waves had come before he could get down to his car and had trapped him in his building. At that time of day, he knew his mother would've been at his familial home in Ryoishi. Past tsunamis had wiped out the low-lying district, and the city had built a two-story seawall, but would it have been enough? His brother would've been at work, and, in her seventies, with her bad legs, his mother would have had trouble getting out of the house and up the hills on her own. If only he could see her and know she was safe.

He wasn't the only one kept awake by images glimpsed during the tsunami. As the night settled over them, he heard sad moans rising from the figures sprawled across the floor. He wandered through his own terrors in the dark, and the morning brought little relief.

In the early light, the members of the neighborhood association, who'd assumed responsibility for the emergency shelter, began organizing the refugees—designating leadership roles, writing down responsibilities on the classroom's blackboard. One group was in charge of cleaning the bathrooms, another was responsible for food disbursement, and so on. As part of the cooking crew Keitaro helped set up the cook stoves, under the supervision of another refugee named Marufuji, who was a local restaurateur. The first day after the tsunami, everyone was given one bowl of rice and a cup of miso soup. At least it was something.

When his duties were taken care of, Keitaro decided to go have a look at the building where he'd had his salon, where he'd rented an apartment for more than two decades. The elementary school sat on top of a small hill in the inland, eastern side of the city; it was only a few blocks from the bottom of the school's drive to his salon, but he had to pick his way through the mud and debris. It was cold out, and he was freezing by the time he arrived at what had been the main shopping street.

Along the waterfront, the enormous steel mill, which usually bustled with cars and trucks sending plumes of steam into the air, was deserted and still. The stink was awful. The smell of rotten fish filled his nose, and his shoes were slick with the same foul black mud that had coated everything. He could hardly tell the difference between the sidewalks, the roads, and the empty spaces where buildings had once stood. Of course, no one was out shopping or waiting for the city bus on the main road; the road was impassable, and no cars or trucks hummed past him. It didn't even seem like a town to him anymore.

He spotted his own building and saw that the entry door was gone. He remembered seeing it in pieces, floating in the water that had filled the stairwell. He crossed the street, thinking he'd climb the steps and get a look at this salon, but the entry was covered with silt. Already cold, he'd only get dirty and likely hurt himself climbing to the second floor. What he found up there wouldn't do anything to dispel the depression descending upon him.

He turned back without checking on his rooms or his workspace, where, for years, he'd cut hair and chatted with his customers.

March 14

The day before, supplies had finally reached the shelter. A dull-green Self-Defense Forces truck had rolled into the elementary school's grounds, and troops in helmets and fatigues hopped down and began handing out rice balls and bowls of miso soup.

Keitaro joined the refugees rushing outside. It was as if the soldiers had come to liberate Kamaishi from some evil occupying force; they handed out rice balls and bowls of miso soup, and, for the first time since the tsunami, the evacuation area had felt connected to the world again.

Not long after the soldiers had arrived, Keitaro went back inside. He was walking through the school's hallway when, as if in a dream, he saw his older brother. He stood looking at his brother and was filled with the all the complex, conflicted feelings of their relationship.

As with so many siblings, Keitaro's relationship with his brother was not without its complications. When they were younger, his brother had been an athlete; he'd excelled in rugby, one of the most popular sports in Kamaishi, where Nippon Steel had once sponsored a team that played in the professional rugby union league. His early fortune had foretold the success he'd have as an adult: after finishing school, he'd found a job with SMC, a large machinery company, gotten married, had a couple of boys, and taken over as the head of the Matsumoto household. Meanwhile, Keitaro had moved away to Sendai in his youth and had struggled to find stability. Eventually, he'd learned his trade as a stylist and returned to Kamaishi to set up his own shop.

While life had taken them on different paths, they were still family. A flash of recognition froze them in their tracks, but they didn't hug or shake hands.

"I'm glad you're alive," his brother said.

"Yeah, I'm okay," Keitaro said. "And you?"

Both he and his wife had been safely at work when the disaster struck, and their grown son lived inland, in the city of Morioka. His brother had taken refuge at his wife's younger sister's house, and, that morning, he'd borrowed an SUV from a friend to come to Kamaishi and search the shelters for a close friend of his from Ryoishi. It was only by chance that he'd run into Keitaro.

Keitaro didn't want to bother his brother and was going to let him resume searching for his hometown friend, but he had to ask what had happened to their mother. It turned out his brother didn't know either. They made plans to drive out to Ryoishi the next day before saying goodbye.

Three days after the disaster, late in the morning, they climbed into the borrowed SUV and pulled out of the elementary school's parking lot. They couldn't take the highway to Ryoishi, as the tunnel that passed under the mountains was closed until it could be checked to make sure it was safe and hadn't suffered any damage in the quake. Instead, his brother drove them up into the old, narrow mountain road that had connected the hamlet to Kamaishi since before the highway had been built.

Both of them knew what must've happened to Ryoishi, and this premonition, as well as their fatigue, bound them both in silence. Less than a kilometer as the crow flies from the hamlet, just as they came out of the last tunnel before Ryoishi, there was a giant crack in the road as if the asphalt had been slashed with a knife and pressed down on one side.

His bother stopped the car, and they got out and stepped over the crack. In front of them, the road was gone—the asphalt had sunk and collapsed.

Instead, they had to hike up the dirt track that went up the hill to the south of Ryoishi. The hamlet was built in a v-shaped valley, with the wide end facing the ocean; the massive seawall guarded the semicircular coast and most the homes were crammed into the lowlands between the steep rises on either side. The path up the backside of the hill was steep and overgrown, and the two brothers could barely make their way forward.

When they came to where they could look down into the valley, Keitaro saw the destruction of his home: Ryoishi was gone. The waves had left nothing that could be recognized as a village. Of the more than two hundred homes, only a dozen or so still stood near the back of the valley or on low hills. The other houses had all been pulverized. He could hardly recognize where his own home should have been. The waves had pushed over the thick concrete panels of the seawall, leaving them toppled over like a child's forgotten building blocks. The outline of the road was completely lost to the confusion of the rubble: a downed concrete telephone pole, a capsized boat, a plastic bathtub, a fragment of a roof. On the stone cliff below the hamlet's Shinto shrine, he even saw a lifeless human arm.

The Matsumoto brothers had come looking for their mother, but as soon as Keitaro saw the ruins, he knew they wouldn't find her there. The disaster had ruined everything in Ryoishi, and even his love for his mother—the common but profound love of a son for the woman who'd shared her talent for cooking with him, showed him how to cook eggs in sweet soy sauce, how to chop spinach and fry it in the pan—turned into pain. Neither he nor his brother spoke. What was there to say?

Once they couldn't stand looking at the wreckage anymore, they turned and walked back to the SUV. The afternoon was growing late as they drove back along their route to the elementary school. They said goodbye in the parking lot, and it would be the last Keitaro saw of his brother for a while. In the coming weeks and months, they'd both be busy with the business of getting up and moving forward day by day.

March 15

Keitaro made the chilly walk down into the inundation zone, went to his old building, and climbed the stairs to his salon.

Inside, everything was a mess. It was exactly as it had been when he'd left four days before: dirty footprints on the floor, glass from the broken window crunching beneath his shoes, the heater in the middle of the room where he and the other survivors had warmed themselves as the tsunami receded. He brought the little kit with his scissors, combs, and razors with him, and he took these tools out and laid them on the counter.

It was less than a week since the tsunami, but he already missed being in his salon. He'd seen to his family as best he could, and, with supplies arriving at the elementary school, there wasn't much he could do in the evacuation area. Tired of his own thoughts, he wanted to work. He remembered how, over three decades before, after the Miyagi Earthquake, the Queen Salon in Sendai, where he'd learned his trade, had reopened only a few days later, as people were still cleaning up the damage and trying to ascertain the impact. Being open for business had buoyed the local people; not just because they could come to get their haircut, but because it gave them a sense that not everything was lost—that life would someday return to normal.

Keitaro had seen other people poking around the ruins of the Kamaishi's shopping districts. No one had time to do their hair anymore—everyone went around brushing long bangs out of their eyes as they searched through the rubble; dyed hair growing out to reveal black or gray roots. He'd had his first bath just a day before—in front of Kamaishi Station, the Self-Defense Forces had set up an enormous communal tub enclosed in a drab-green tent—and he remembered how much better he felt to experience such a simple luxury again.

The electricity in Hair Studio K was dead, and when he turned the tap on the sink no water came out. He had his scissors though. He had a broom and dustpan; he had his empty salon chair facing the mirror on the wall, and, for eight or nine hours each day, he had enough light to work by. He set about making a sign to post outside. He usually charged an amount that was high but not unreasonable for a stylist who took his time with each customer. Considering the limitations to his services though, he slashed his fee in half. In red marker, on a piece of plain white paper, he wrote: *Offering cuts only! 2,000 yen!*

He posted this sign outside his door and then sat down to wait.

April 12

After reopening his salon, Keitaro had given cuts to over five-hundred customers. Many were regular clients, who'd been glad to see him back in business, but others were first-time customers—they'd seen the sign and were in need of a cut. A reporter from the *Asahi Shinbun* newspaper had even come to interview him for an article about life in the disaster-affected zone.

He was still living in a classroom on the first floor of the elementary school, still unable to see more than a week or so into the future. He'd managed to charge his phone, but there was no one he needed to contact. He'd seen his brother, and his mother was still missing. He prayed for her, hoping she might still be found alive somewhere.

A month after the tsunami, Yanagida Masato, a friend of his who was also vice principal of the nearby Odaira Middle School, had asked Keitaro if he could come and give haircuts to the refugees in his facility. Everyone's hair had grown out, and he might see as many as twenty clients in one session at Odaira. He'd also begun cutting the hair of the survivors at Kamaishi Elementary.

At both schools, he would lay out a tarp in the gymnasium and put a chair in the middle. Working without electric clippers or a blow dryer, there was only so much he could do, but he soon grew used to working as a barber. The soreness he'd felt in his hands the first few days quickly disappeared. It wasn't much, but it felt good to work again. He didn't think of trying to set a price or charge a fee, but sometimes people would offer him a few coins or crumpled bills for his services.

Having been through the tsunami himself, he knew better than to try to talk to his customers about the disaster and, instead, asked them about their everyday lives—the things that felt like normal life. All the hair he was cutting now was from before the tsunami, and, with each snip of his scissors, he cut away one more strand of the past.

Relief, Recovery

May-July 2011

I. Of God and Water

Mutsu City, Aomori Prefecture

In a booth in McDonald's, I dialed my mother's cell phone over and over on Skype. In her email, Mom had written that it was an emergency—I should call as soon as possible.

I had come north to see Junko, and, the next day, I was heading to Iwate Prefecture to do my first stint as a volunteer in Kamaishi City. Over the past few days, I'd met up with the other foreign teachers who'd been my coworkers when I'd taught English there and had eaten dinner with the group of middle-aged women who'd taught me how to cook back when I didn't know how to boil an egg. It had been a year since I'd returned to the US for graduate school, but the city hadn't changed a bit. It seemed the disaster hadn't affected anything this far north.

I'd brought my computer bag in order to do some writing and check my email because the fast food restaurant was one of the only places in Mutsu with Wi-Fi at the time. When I opened my inbox, the first thing I saw was a message from my mom, who said she was at Sea-Tac airport about to get on a plane to Cleveland—my eighty-seven-year-old grandfather's health was going and going fast.

It didn't make any sense. I was in a master's program at Ohio State, and, just a month ago, I'd finished grading the final essays of the class I was teaching, submitted my own last assignments for the graduate seminar I was taking, and made the two-hour trip from Columbus to Cleveland where my grandparents lived. Grandpa had been in a rehabilitation center, but, after a trying spring, his heart condition was finally under control. I'd stayed with my grandmother and uncle for a few days, then got on a plane at Hopkins International Airport and headed to Seattle, where I visited my parents for a week, before flying to Tokyo.

Now, in the McDonald's, I reread my mom's email. It was twelve hours old, so I figured she'd have touched down in Ohio by then. I bent my head down, my ear turned toward my laptop's speakers. I listened to her phone's ring and worried I wouldn't hear her pick up over the shrieks of laughter echoing out of the Play Place. She answered the third time I called and told me she was at the Hospice of Western Reserve. Things weren't looking good.

"He went for a checkup yesterday and his blood toxins were through the roof," she said. "He hadn't been able to pee for a week and didn't tell anyone."

There was a sob in her last word, and something in my throat pinched as well. The smell of grilled beef and deep-frying, a smell common to

McDonald's the world over, surrounded me like a dismal fog. My mom was a nurse practitioner with forty years of experience; if anyone could diagnose the end of life, she could. I was used to her calling me from Washington with smaller concerns about Grandpa's health. It was easy to dismiss these little worries, but her being at the hospice with him was different.

"Should I come home?" I asked, thinking about my Visa card's bloated balance. The price of another airline ticket was well above my credit limit.

"Oh, no. You probably wouldn't make it anyway. He'd be proud of what you're doing over there." Shame warmed through me like a fever. After landing in Tokyo a couple weeks earlier, I'd taken a bullet train three hours due north and bypassed the disaster area. I'd worked on a garlic farm for a couple weeks during the harvest season, making some money to pay my expenses. Since I'd arrived on the Shimokita Peninsula, I hadn't done anything but go out for drinks with my friends and try to make up for lost time with Junko. "They have him on a lot of pain meds," my mom said. "He's only woken up once since I've been here."

By then my mom was openly crying. I covered my mouth with my hand and struggled to hear her over the fast-food din. I'd ordered a cheeseburger so the staff wouldn't get mad at me for taking up a table. I'd eaten it before I read my mom's email, and, as I listened to her weeping into the phone, my stomach felt heavy with guilt and processed food. Even before I'd asked, I'd known I wasn't going back.

"I'm sorry I can't be there," I said. "I thought he was getting better."

"I did too." The garbled sound of a PA announcement passed through the background. "It just seems like it's his time."

We talked for a few more minutes, repeating the clichés people use to discuss death and dying. Really, I think we just needed to listen to the sound of each other's voices a little longer. Before we hung up, I asked her to text me any updates and explained how she could message me on the cheap rental cell phone Junko had arranged for me to pick up at the airport in Tokyo.

I packed up my computer, left McDonald's, and headed toward the English Conversation Club, or ECC, a private cram school where I'd been sleeping at night. It was owned by Nakanishi-*san*, one of the women I'd met through weekly cooking classes that were held in a community center in Mutsu. When I'd first moved to Shimokita, she was one of the few people I met who spoke English, and she'd helped me get settled. Though I'd minored in Japanese, my language skills had been shaky—I hadn't planned on living in the country until a professor at my college told me about the Japan Exchange and Teaching Programme.

With the American economy in a downturn, the job market for new graduates had been bleak and the chance to go abroad sounded exciting.

Back then, being overseas had made sense. But, as I thought about my grandfather dying in Ohio, I questioned my decision to return. Junko was here, but, with her father's condition, she'd said, and I'd agreed, it wasn't the right time to introduce me to her family. I couldn't stay at her house, and we hadn't had much time together.

The sky was darkening overhead, and the streetlights flickered on as I thought about the last time I'd been with my grandparents. I'd taken the Greyhound from Columbus to Cleveland and then got on a Laketran bus out toward Willowick, one of the city's eastern suburbs. In the spring, while he was putting the storm windows away, Grandpa had taken a bad fall, broken a couple ribs, and wound up with internal bleeding and a prescription for three months of inpatient rehab. The day after I arrived, my uncle Russ drove my grandmother and me out to the Heartland of Mentor post-hospital care center. Lying in bed, in his t-shirt and sweatpants, Grandpa looked thin, diminished even. But my uncle said he'd gained weight, which was good. Before his fall, he'd had digestion problems, but since then they'd had him on a steady diet of fiber-filled meals, laxatives, and physical therapy.

Russ suggested we take Grandpa outside, saying the walk would do him good. I held his lukewarm catheter bag while he got out of bed, hooked it to his walker once he was on his feet, and then the four of us shuffled down the hall.

The day had been bright, and the last of the afternoon sun poured down on two wooden benches that flanked the entry. It was pastoral, in its own institutional way. My grandfather sat with his wife on one bench, Russ and I sat across from them, and we talked about how the Indians couldn't possibly hang onto their lead in the American League Central—which, of course, they didn't—how Ford had stopped making Grandpa's favorite car, the Crown Victorian, and how soon the bugs would start coming in off Lake Erie.

That was the last time I saw my grandfather. The last time I looked him in the eye and noticed the fumbling way he adjusted his glasses, the way his potato-shaped nose quivered when he laughed. A month later, I was alone in one of the ECC classrooms in Mutsu, an ocean away, as his presence leaked out of the world. It felt stupid and maudlin to cry alone, but I couldn't help myself as I spread a futon pad on the floor. I wouldn't have said my grandfather and I were exceptionally close, but he was part of my life and one of the reasons I'd moved back to Ohio for graduate school. Now, I would never again sit with him and ask him to tell me how he'd nearly died on the Siegfried Line on a cold day in 1944—never again would I watch him read the front page of *The Plain Dealer* with a magnifying glass, or hear him play polkas on his electric organ. All of that was gone.

Junko opened the door to the cram school and found me wiping my eyes. Though I felt guilty over inviting her to the room Nakanishi-*san* had let me stay in, we were desperate and had agreed it would be nice to spend my last night in Mutsu together. But, as I explained about Grandpa to her, I was a wreck. We squeezed together onto a single futon pad, and she put her arms around me. I told her the things I remembered about Grandpa, and, talking to her, I could almost forget he was dying.

Then, the reality that he'd soon be utterly, totally gone would come rushing back, and I'd feel as though I was being sucked into the floor. Junko held me, ran her fingers through my hair, and told me it would be okay. But I knew it wouldn't.

July 18

The next morning, Junko left early. Not long after, I hefted my backpack onto my shoulders and walked to the train station. It wasn't easy to leave, but I'd be back in a month or so. Besides, Junko needed to be with her family: her father's condition had taken a turn for worse in recent months. He'd been released from the hospital, but, every couple days, her mom still took him to Aomori City for chemotherapy, a two-hour drive each way. Junko, her sister, and her mother were busy caring for her father, running her family's cosmetics shop, and taking care of their two dogs. It was all hands on deck.

As I waited for the local train at Shimokita Station, I thought about Junko, who I'd come all this way to see. I was beginning to realize, with everything that was happening, we might not make it through all this. I wanted some sign that I'd made the right choices, but I didn't see anything.

When I arrived in Hachinohe, a city in the south of the prefecture, I sprinted through the station to make my transfer to the southbound Shinkansen. After two stops, I got off in Morioka and boarded a bus Junko had said would take me east to Kamaishi City on the Pacific coast.

I took a seat near the back of the bus and soon fell asleep. When I woke an hour later, we were driving up a curving road in the hills of Iwate Prefecture. I closed my eyes and leaned against the window, but my head bounced against the glass every time the bus lurched through one of the sharp cutbacks. I sat up, flipped open my cell, and found a message from my mom:

Dad is very short of breath and getting oxygen. He said the hospice is good... It's a beautiful facility on the lakefront with gardens all around. There is a baby across the hall that is tiny and has a very small head without much brain and is being kept comfortable until death...He has stopped making urine, so likely hours to a couple of days until he passes. Over and over he kept saying, 'Life is so good, but dying is terrible.' The pastor stopped by this morning, so I know that Dad has comfort in his faith. This is the hardest thing I have ever been through...

Since early that morning I'd been preoccupied with train schedules and station maps, but my mother's words brought me back to what our family was going through.

Loss had barely touched my life up until then, and the sting was unlike anything I'd ever felt. Before then, the closest person to me who'd died was a boy in middle school who'd had brain cancer. Though we'd gotten in a fight once on the playground when we were children, this hadn't led to any lasting animosity or friendship; we weren't close, though I attended the memorial service along with nearly everyone else in my tiny hometown. I was too young then to think of grief as anything more than a pose, a stance I adopted in imitation of the real mourners.

Nearly two decades later, the bus rocked back and forth, and I felt dazed by my first real brush with true loss. Unable to wrap my head around the tone of finality in my mother's message, I did my best to let the passing landscape fill my mind. Outside, the lush valleys of Tohoku were as beautiful a view as I'd ever seen: rice paddies grew up the hills in terraced steps until the old forests took over; a faint gauze of smoke hung in the air from the fires the farmers had set in their fields.

When the bus reached the outskirts of Kamaishi, I started to look for the ruins I'd seen in the news broadcasts—cars hanging out of windows, ships balanced on rooftops. But I didn't spot a single collapsed building, not one cracked pane of glass. A sense of normalcy hung in the narrow alleys between the sturdy but weather-beaten houses.

I got off the bus at a stop across from the enormous factory that dominated half the port district; the words *Nippon Steel* were painted on one tall, sheet-metal building. The whole complex constantly belched steam into the air and the many teal buildings were linked by elevated tracks and pipes. I imagined liquefied metals being pumped from one structure to another like a giant intravenous system. Looking at the compound more closely, in a field near the center of the mill, I saw a pile of detritus two-stories tall. Chunks of roofing material, splintered wood, and shreds of clothing were heaped together in a mound as big as several houses, though nowhere did I see the devastation that had produced the debris. It seemed all the rubble had been collected there—the entire city had been cleaned up before I'd arrived. I was missing my grandfather's final days to be here, and yet there wasn't a scrap of wreckage anywhere in sight.

I forced down my disappointment, took out a map that Junko had printed for me before I'd left Mutsu, and started toward the Caritas Base where I'd registered to volunteer.

Kamaishi was squeezed into a valley, which ran east-to-west toward the ocean. The Koshi River cut through the middle of the valley, and, for a while, I walked along a road following the river's flow. Not far from where the river let out into the bay, the road turned north and took me over a bridge and into the city's shopping district. Immediately, it was clear the waves had reached this quarter.

The facades of the stores along the street had been smashed, their insides coated with black mud. The aluminum siding of some buildings had been cleaved clean off, exposing steel girders and frayed wiring that spilled out like internal organs. A block from the main street, through a hole in the side of a sheet metal warehouse, I spotted the red rectangle of a Coke machine, though the familiar white script was upside down because the vendor had been flipped on its head. Condemned buildings were marked with red Xs, and it seemed about half the buildings in this district had been spray-painted with these crosses. Though I didn't notice it at the time, the building where Keitaro Matsumoto's salon had been was among these.

I instantly multiplied these sights through the complex equation of my emotions, feeling relief at the sight of the silt and broken glass. The evidence of the catastrophe freed me from some of the guilt I felt over not being in Ohio; there was nothing I could've done if I'd been with Grandpa, but, here, I might be of some use.

Before long, I headed up into the hills above the shopping district and wandered the narrow streets until I caught sight of the white Caritas flag in front of two gray buildings. The charity's Kamaishi branch was housed on the grounds of the local Catholic Church, and the volunteer base camp was run out of the two-story rectory across from the sanctuary.

There was no answer when I knocked on the heavy wooden door, so I let myself in, took off my shoes, and left them among the sea of slippers and shoes that crowded the entrance. Despite the flotilla of footwear, there was nobody inside. Then, a thin woman emerged from an office near the front, and the badge hanging from her lanyard around her neck read Ise. Bowing, I introduced myself.

She took me to the men's dorm, leading me through dim halls crowded with stacks of coolers, cardboard boxes of cabbage and daikon, sacks of rice and flour: donations from every corner of the country. Over the next several weeks, I'd learn she'd been a teacher in Kyoto when the disaster struck but had returned to her hometown, where her family had long been part of the Catholic community, to help with the volunteer effort. As she showed me the men's quarters, I could tell by the way she moved—stepping over boxes, knowing how every door opened—that she was in charge.

I dropped my backpack in the sleeping area and followed her upstairs to the dining room. At one of the tables was a man who looked to be in his mid-thirties, a newspaper in his hands and a cup of coffee by his elbow, his tan, wrinkleless features fixed in an expression just shy of a smile. He stood and we bowed. Ise introduced me to Hiramatsu, a long-term volunteer who helped manage the base. Setting his paper aside, he took me in with a glance.

"The others have left for the day," he said. "But I have some errands to run. After lunch, I could take you around."

The trip had sapped my energy, but my instinct was to get started right away, to throw myself into the volunteer effort and let the work overwhelm my emotions and my thoughts. I felt encouraged by meeting Hiramatsu—his attention was so focused, like a solid thing that pressed into you without prying. My own thoughts and feelings were like countless loose ends spilling out of me, and I wanted to work, to grind myself down to a point like him.

A woman with a scarf tied over her white hair came staggering out of the kitchen, carrying a stockpot nearly as big as she was. She put the pot down on a table set against the wall and the tray of glasses next to it rattled against each other.

"Sister, this is Michael. He came from America," Ise said. "Sister Ozawa is from Tokyo."

Ise later explained about the Sister's Relay, in which nuns from all over the country did one-month rotations at churches in the tsunami-affected area. Sister Ozawa had been in Kamaishi for a couple weeks when I arrived. I'd always respected monks, nuns, and clergymen for the faith their vocations required, and part of me wondered what the sister knew about the passage my grandfather was about to make.

She looked up at me through her glasses, wiped her hands on her apron, and said something in her sweet, whistling voice that I was hopeless to understand.

I shook my head, and she waved to the pot: "Go ahead, please eat."

The smell of curry was spreading through the room, and my hunger perked up. I'd planned on grabbing lunch on the way to Kamaishi, but my mother's message had tamped down my appetite. Now, I realized how hungry I was, how ready I was to let this place fill me up.

"Sure," I said. "I could eat."

After lunch, I went downstairs with Hiramatsu, and he issued me a name tag, a lanyard, and a neon-green vest to identify me as a Caritas volunteer. We went over a list of guidelines about safety in the disaster area and the kind of work I was allowed to do. I understood most of what he said and nodded my way through the rest. There were always a lot of rules. I'd learned if you obeyed all of them, you'd never get anywhere. Besides, the most important parts were common sense: no wandering out into the wreckage on your own, no taking souvenirs or photos without permission.

Having finished my orientation, I followed Hiramatsu outside, and we got in a sedan with a basketball-sized Caritas sticker on the hood. He drove us north out of the city, his eyes fixed to a spot on the windshield an arm's length in front of him. He drove the same way he talked, his movements steady, quiet, and exceedingly smooth. After a few minutes, we entered a series of tunnels, which ran under the hills separating Kamaishi City from Otsuchi, the neighboring municipality. In the dark, his attention on the road, I began to ask him about himself.

Shadows played over his face as he answered my questions: he was from Tokyo, it was his first time in Tohoku, and, no, he wasn't Catholic. This wasn't surprising; Caritas welcomed volunteers of all faiths, and less than one percent of the country was Catholic. He'd heard of the opportunity to be a long-term volunteer at the base camp through a friend.

Before I could ask more, we emerged from the tunnel, and the highway off-ramp curved to the right, leading us down toward the sea and what was left of the town of Otsuchi. Ahead of us, the remaining buildings could be counted on one hand. Nothing under two stories was still standing. Of the buildings that hadn't been washed away, most had been stripped of their siding; their rusted steel frames were skeletal pillars towering over the coastal plain. All the other structures had been smashed and scattered by the waves. The area resembled a massive landfill: mixed in with the black earth were crumbs of sheetrock, shards of plastic, shiny bits of aluminum. Other than a few weeds, the low-lying areas had been stripped of each root, every blade of grass.

Like Kamaishi, the town was spread out across a valley, which opened toward the ocean. When I looked close, I could see aspects of a typical port town twisted through the lens of disaster: a white fishing boat balanced on a bare foundation; an entire station gone, save for the platforms, where passengers would've stood as the local Yamada Line train pulled in. Where the coastal plain met the hilly forests, the cedars had died, their needles turning red after the poison salt water seeped into their roots and their crimson color marking how far the waves had reached. Against the base of one foothill, a station wagon had been crushed like an egg in a strong grip and deposited next to part of a tiled wall. The damage in this town was of a different order than what I'd seen in Kamaishi—entire districts were gone, wiped out.

I was stunned and silent.

As Hiramatsu drove he talked about how the Self-Defense Forces were the ones who'd cleared the roads. Around us, debris-filled dump trucks rumbled down the streets and police officers directed traffic at intersections. An orange bus with the Japan Post logo on it served as the town's makeshift mail center. We entered what had once been the town's central district, and I spotted three buildings hung with handmade banners showing Otsuchi's pixie-like mascot and bearing messages of hope and perseverance: *Thanks forever! Keep fighting Otsuchi!* The signs were fashioned from blue tarps decorated with colored tape, and they looked like the flags of some battered army.

In the distance, the calm port was visible, and, looking at the glass sheet of Otsuchi Bay, I reminded myself that the sea and the ruins were related—one had caused the other—and the power that had produced such destruction still lay beneath the surface.

We pulled up to a four-story building, and Hiramatsu said the Kamaishi Base was going to start sending volunteers to work there tomorrow. He'd come to get a look so he'd know what tools they'd need. We parked, and he pointed out a deformed plastic sign, which had melted from the heat of a fire that had burned through the buildings across the street. Though they were warped, I could make out the characters: *Hotel Kotobuki.*

I followed him inside and he told me the owner had asked for Caritas' help in turning the hotel into a base camp where volunteers could stay while they worked in what was left of Otsuchi. The building was structurally sound, he said, and other than a four-month coating of dust the guest rooms on the third and fourth floors were in good shape. But the first two floors had been soaked in a mixture of mud, sewage, dead fish, and all the chemicals the waves had picked up and churned together. Everything needed to be torn out—the water-damaged wood, the drywall, the tile ceilings—and the concrete underneath had to be pressure washed.

Back in the car, Hiramatsu said he was going to take me to a photo-cleaning project, where a group of volunteers was sorting through pictures found in the wreckage to return them to the survivors. He drove toward the hills, and, as we left the coast behind, I asked what he did for a living.

"I'm not working now," he said. "Just volunteering."

I realized I might've embarrassed him with my question; in a country where lifetime employment was once the norm and exchanging business cards is one of the first things people do upon meeting, joblessness carried a stigma.

I tried to regain some ground, asking, "What were you doing before the tsunami?"

"I didn't have a job. I used to work with computers, but that was a while ago."

I nodded, falling silent. In 1991, the asset bubble had burst, and since then the country had experienced the Lost Decades, twenty years with little economic growth. In 2008, just as the country seemed ready to turn the corner, the Lehman Crash and ensuing global downturn plunged the economy back into recession. Even well-qualified people were having trouble finding work.

I wasn't going to say anything more, but Hiramatsu didn't seem bothered and asked how I'd learned Japanese. "What brought you here?"

I'd been asked this question a hundred times and had several answers worked out for it, though the actual reasons I'd come so many times were not so simple. For one, I enjoyed the distance and sense of perspective on my own culture that living abroad gave me. I also loved the exactness of Japan, the buses that ran on time to the minute and the spotless city streets, which contrasted brilliantly with my own internal chaos. And, of course, during my first visits to the country as a student, everything had been new and interesting and alluring: the strange but delicious food, the reserved sensibility of the men and women. After I'd come to live in the country, everything gradually stopped seeming so exotic, and this allowed me to see the people I met for the individuals they were. The friends I made in Mutsu, especially the members of my cooking class, were centered, calm, and possessed a kind of practical wisdom. Unlike me, they didn't dread or expect too much of the world. They didn't spend their days anxious or worrying—as I did—if they were on the right track, if they were accomplishing enough. They simply lived, a way I envied.

Instead of this, I told Hiramatsu how, when I'd studied abroad in a Chiba Prefecture, I'd had a warm, generous homestay family, who I'd kept in touch with ever since. I still visited the Gokitas whenever I arrived, and my memories of staying up late, eating peanuts, and drinking *shochu* with Mr. G were some of the first to come to mind every time I booked a flight to Narita International Airport. This was true, of course, though it was a smaller truth.

We'd been on the road for about half an hour when Hiramatsu turned off the highway, following the signs for a district of Kamaishi called Hashino. We pulled up to an elementary school, and I saw its walls were streaked with black mold; tufts of tall grass had sprouted on the roof as though the building was growing hair. It was clear the school had been out of use since before the disaster, a testament to how communities in the area had aged and shrank; since a few years before the tsunami, the country's population had been contracting, and small cities and towns had been hit hard as young people, uninterested in farming or the declining manufacturing trades like Kamaishi's shrinking steel industry, moved to cities like Tokyo or Sendai.

Hiramatsu led me to a dim gymnasium at the north end of the grounds. Inside, thousands of cleaned photos were arranged on tables beneath the rusting basketball hoops; near the door, laundry baskets of dirt-caked pictures, which had been culled from the wreckage, were stacked shoulder high.

Making my bows, I introduced myself to the people who were overseeing the project and the Caritas volunteers who'd been there since the morning. The man in charge of the operation showed me to a table and handed me a stack of photos. Hiramatsu said his goodbyes and I pulled on a pair of latex gloves and got to work wiping dried mud from pictures, looking for identifying information, putting them in order by family or company name.

The tsunami had scattered refugees all over the country; contacting survivors to tell them their pictures had been found wasn't feasible, but notices about the project had been posted in village offices. Once in a while, someone would wander in, pick over the tables, and claim a few photos, evidence of a past that had otherwise been washed away.

In the first stack of photos I cleaned, I came across a print of a mustached white man wearing a black suit, standing in front of a chalkboard with an American flag drawn on it and looking out on a classroom of children in blue tracksuits. The man was obviously an English teacher in a school, which I eventually learned had been destroyed by the tsunami. Later on, I brushed dirt from an album of prints of a young woman, and, from her clothes and the cars in the pictures, it seemed it'd been taken in the 80s. The pictures were of her at a table holding a glass of caramel-colored liquor, her throwing her head back in laughter, her smoking a cigarette at a party in a cocktail dress and lipstick so, so red—her in a car's passenger seat in nothing but her underwear. The way she smiled, the angle of the pictures, everything about them made me think her lover had been behind the camera. They would be middle-aged now, old even, and I wondered if they'd stayed together, if they'd survived all this.

The other volunteers and I finished our last photos around four in the afternoon and wiped down our tables. I rode back in the car that the rest of the Caritas members had come in that morning. We followed the winding highway between the mountains, a quiet hanging between us, and the only sound was the static murmur of a voice on the radio, forecasting a foggy tomorrow.

When we arrived in Kamaishi, the base camp was bustling. It was an entirely different place than it had been in the afternoon. Volunteers stood in the hallways talking on their cell phones while others set off into the night, towels draped over their necks, bottles of shampoo swinging in their grip as they headed to the public bathhouse a couple blocks away. A few of them packed suitcases and said their goodbyes, even as their replacements arrived, hands full of pillows and *omiyage* souvenirs they'd brought. The more veteran volunteers caught each other in the dorms or gathered around the ashtrays outside to chat about the day's work, and these scenes of togetherness reminded me of my family—my mother, aunt, uncle, and their cousins, who would've been gathering around my grandparents' house in Cleveland, someone sleeping on the couch, someone waiting for the shower.

I went to the bathhouse, had a soak, and by the time I returned the base camp's nightly meeting was about to begin. Two-dozen volunteers gathered in the women's dorm, the biggest room in the rectory, and we sat in a circle on the carpet. Ise and Sister Ozawa sat near Hiramatsu, who started by asking for self-introductions from the new arrivals. A Filipino woman introduced herself and her daughter, saying they'd come in connection with the church they belonged to. After she finished, Hiramatsu turned to me.

I explained myself haltingly, saying I was a graduate student in the US but had lived in Aomori Prefecture before. Keeping it short, I talked about my gratitude to the people of Tohoku and how I hoped I could do something to repay their kindness.

This was true enough, but it hardly explained why I'd come so far to sort through wreckage and pick out the mementos of other people's lives. Though I couldn't articulate it at the time, the years I'd taught English in Mutsu had steadied me; I'd made friends and come to feel at home there, and this had helped me decide to pursue my writing. As the meeting moved on to updates of the projects the base camp had dispatched volunteers to, I was certain only that I felt a deep sense of connection to the area. Part of it was my stubborn sentimentality and part, of course, was Junko. I had wanted to come back, and the disaster had given shape to my return.

In preparation for the next day, Hiramatsu held up a piece of poster paper with all the volunteer projects written on it and asked everyone to sign up for a project. Then he turned to Sister Ozawa and asked her if she would bring the meeting to a close.

"Dear Lord," she began, inclining her head in prayer.

I lowered my eyes. Though my dad had been raised Catholic and my mother Protestant, except for the Christmas service my mom and I attended every year, I'd been brought up outside organized religion. After college, equally repelled by the dogmatic atheists and strident spiritualists I'd met, or whose work I'd read, I settled into a wishy-washy agnosticism. Considering how little we understood of existence, denying the possibility of anything greater than humanity seemed foolish. But my belief in—or, more accurately, hope for—something indefinable wasn't at all satisfying. So, once I started graduate school in Columbus, I began wandering down to the church on the same block as my apartment a few times each month. I would drink cup after cup of coffee and eat a couple donuts while I listened to the portly pastor's sermon.

Going to King Avenue United Methodist Church had also been a way of connecting with the Midwestern culture of my mother and grandparents. I'd loved living in Japan, but the country wasn't a singular obsession for me; I'd wanted to explore the world and hadn't planned on becoming so attached to one particular corner of it. When I moved to Ohio, I was still in the searching years of my life, and something as conventional as waking up early on Sunday and tucking a collared shirt into a clean pair of khakis was so unlike the way I was used to spending my weekends that it practically seemed like an adventure. The congregation was a mix of young and middle-aged people, including a quite a few gay men; all of them were plain, friendly Midwesterners, open to anyone who wandered in.

No matter how many sermons I listened to though, I couldn't align my thinking with the Christian idea of faith. I'd always done well in school, and probably because of this I approached everything in my life as though like it was a course I was taking. I related to the world through knowledge. Faith, as far as I could tell, was about foreswearing knowledge, something I felt incapable of, especially when it came to the most worrying matters, such as death, meaning, and the essence of our selves. Still, I admired those who believed, like Sister Ozawa. In her email, my mother had said my grandfather had found comfort in his faith, and I hoped this was true. For my part, I couldn't say if I believed in God, heaven, or such a thing as a soul. But, in that moment, I wanted to.

I lowered my head and silently prayed my grandfather would be at peace.

July 19

I woke early and lay half-asleep in my futon, drifting in and out of dreams of northern Ohio.

Though I'd heard my aunt, uncle, grandparents, and mother all talk about the bitterness of Northeastern winters—lake-effect snow and icebreakers cleaving open shipping lanes to the Erie Canal—in my mind, it was always summer in the suburbs east of Cleveland. During the hot months in Willowick, there was a smell of wet clay and heat, the many blooming trees and piles of dead midges, the freshly mowed grass. These scents mixed into a single rich aroma and hung over the neighborhood from June until mid-September. Because I associated this smell with my grandparents, to me it was the smell of old people. When I was a boy and would come with my mother on trips to the house where she'd grown up, I'd stand on the steps outside the kitchen door, take in the long backyard, and inhale nosefuls of the foreign air.

Near the back edge of the yard there was a small, fenced-off square where my grandfather had his vegetable patch. In the hour before night descended and the fireflies appeared, I remember watching him while he pushed his rototiller up the five-yard rows, and the machine's metal blades turned the earth. Later, at the kitchen table, when darkness had filled the windows, his hands shook as he opened that day's chamber in his pillbox and dumped out his blood pressure and heart medications. He caught me staring and said, "My hands are still rototilling," then washed down his pills with a drink of iced tea.

My grandfather loved gardening. He'd been raised on a farm in Amish country, and he'd loved the earth and things that grew. I remember him driving us out into the cornfields in Geauga County in the Crown Vic, looking for a particular produce stand he liked. We'd talk about anything—what I was studying at school or the car trips he'd used to make down to Florida. Or maybe I was mixing things up, and maybe it had actually been me driving and Grandpa was older than I was thinking.

As I lay in my bedding on the floor of the men's dorm in Kamaishi, I struggled to hold onto the memory, but it grew hazier as I grappled with it until it faded entirely. By half-past six, the light was too bright to ignore any longer. I threw aside the covers and went up to the dining room.

In the kitchen, still in his linen pajamas, Hiramatsu was making coffee. In order to make a kettle of coffee big enough for the entire base camp, he'd engineered a dripper out of four arm-length metal rods, which held in place an enormous filter packed with coffee. From a teapot, Hiramatsu poured steaming water over the grounds, and it trickled down into a pumpkin-shaped kettle resting on the floor. Once he'd poured all the water, he took a plastic bucket from under the sink and began sifting through the sand-colored paste inside with the blade of a paring knife, picking out pickled carrots, eggplants, and cucumbers. He sliced them on a cutting board with his eyes half closed.

Still groggy with sleep myself, I turned and went to the dining room, where I sat at a table with a man with a shaved-bald head whom I hadn't met the day before. In Tohoku, custom usually circumscribed social relations between strangers, and, in most cases, I wouldn't have considered sitting with someone I didn't know. But a sense of familiarity permeated the base camp, and I introduced myself to this volunteer without hesitation.

A minute later, Hiramatsu came in with a plate of sliced *tsukemono* and the kettle of coffee. I poured cups for all three of us, took a sip, and complimented Hiramatsu's brew: "Nice and dark, just how I like it."

The bald man smiled at Hiramatsu in a familiar way. "He's weak in the morning. He only makes coffee because he needs it."

Hiramatsu nodded. Still, he was the type who, if he had to have his coffee, would make enough for the whole base; he could run meetings, pickle vegetables, and jury-rig a dripper to fit an industrial-sized kettle. It was hard for me to imagine a man like him had been unemployed before. The skills that had been important before the disaster—fancy degrees, an air of confidence and self-promotion—were of little use in the world the waves had left behind. What was needed here were people who could live without much besides the basic necessities, people who gave more than they took.

From outside, I heard voices and footsteps on the path between the church and the rectory. Mass had started at six in the morning and must have just let out.

"Wherever you go, Catholics do things early," I said.

The bald man said, "And yet they don't have much use for coffee, judging by the stuff Sister Ozawa brews."

We chuckled at this and then lapsed into a silence, enjoying the last of the morning quiet.

A moment later, the other volunteers came up to the dining room for breakfast: rice and soup or a couple slices of buttered toast. At a quarter after seven, all the volunteers once again gathered in the women's dorm. Eyes wide with caffeine, Hiramatsu announced the weather, confirmed where everyone was going and who was driving, and sent us on our way.

Before heading out, we cleaned the base from top to bottom, wiping down the kitchen and vacuuming each room, and then we loaded the church's vehicles with the tools needed for the various projects. At the church, these rituals—the morning meeting, cleaning the base, prepping to go, the nightly meeting when we returned—were repeated every day, and, like the winding of a watch, they set the volunteers on a rhythm.

Along with Takeshi Toyoda, a middle-aged man who'd also signed up to work at the hotel, I helped prep the van going to Otsuchi, checking the shovels, crowbars, hardhats, hammers, extension cords, and first aid kit in the back against a list Hiramatsu had given us. Over the course of several days, I'd learn Takeshi had a family in Sendai and worked in the office of a construction company in the city. He was a quiet, deferential man, unfailingly helpful and easy to work with. He climbed into the driver's seat of the van, and I got in the passenger side.

Despite it being mid-July, the day was gray and misty, and, heading north toward Otsuchi, the van's windshield beaded up with drops of water. The droplets streaked across the glass as we accelerated into the tunnel under the mountains, and I thought about what Junko had said over the phone the night before.

After Sister Ozawa's prayer concluded the evening meeting, I'd called Junko and told her about the people at the base camp, the hotel, and about my mother's email and Grandpa slowly dying in the hospice. She'd said, "He must have been important to you." She was right, in a sense. Part of the reason I'd gone to grad school in Ohio had been to be closer to my grandparents and uncle; I'd hoped doing so could help us make up for lost time. Living in Washington State, six hours by plane from Cleveland, it had been hard to keep in touch. They'd flown out to visit my mother a few times, but I had been too young to remember and knew of these trips only from a picture of Grandpa holding my baby self outside the house on my mother's horse ranch. My grandfather had never particularly liked flying—I think he associated planes with the grim journeys he'd taken during the war—and in his later years, he all but gave up any sort of travel. We'd had a warm relationship, but not a close one.

Time was running out to get to know my grandparents, so when the chance to move to Columbus had come up, I'd taken it. I'd made a couple visits to Cleveland during the school year, sleeping on the bed that folded out of the sofa in the spare room. I'd seen more of Grandpa than I had in a long time, though he wasn't an easy man to get to know. His generation held their opinions close, and, on top of this, the war had left its mark on him. My mother had spent the last four decades of her career nursing in a Veterans Affairs hospital, and she'd said, if Grandpa had come in to see her, she would have diagnosed him with post-traumatic stress. What had he thought of our relationship? Of me? I'd tried to talk to him about the time I'd spent abroad and the ambitions as a writer that so filled me, but I'd never been good at explaining myself.

As we emerged from the tunnels, I realized these were questions I would never have the answers to. To me, life seemed like one long conversation, which, for as long as it continued, held a kind of promise—a cruel phrase could still be apologized for, an impenetrable question could be answered, a forgotten promise might be kept. But death was a sentence cut off. A reply unuttered. Driving through Otsuchi's flattened landscape, I thought about Grandpa and all the voices in the town that had vanished in an instant.

At the derelict hotel, Takeshi and I unloaded the tools and then drifted inside. It fell to him, with his experience in construction, to lead us. He decided we should start with the second-floor restrooms. None of the taps worked, but a pipe had been run in through one of the windows. A spigot above the unusable taps in the sink was our only source of water upstairs.

Takeshi said we'd better get that area cleaned out first, but we could spare the tile and porcelain fixture; the tsunami sludge wouldn't have soaked into those. We had to rip out the false ceilings and the toilet stalls. The wiring on the first two floors was shot, but a power line had been hooked up to a temporary breaker mounted on the outside of the hotel, and the outlets on the third and fourth floors were working. He ran an extension cord down the stairwell and plugged in the pressure washer. We worked in shifts, one of us doing demolition and then the other shoveling out debris or spraying the walls clean. We strapped headlamps on our hard hats, and, if someone had seen us wandering out of the hotel, they probably would've taken us for spelunkers just up from some subterranean cavern.

The work was hard, and we could barely see. Whichever of us wasn't smashing or shoveling or spraying waited outside, catching our breath and wiping off the perspiration inside our protective goggles until the other got tired, staggered out of the dark in a daze, and handed off the crowbar or the shovel or the rifle-like pressure-washer gun. Within a couple of minutes, we were soaked and splattered with mud. By the end of it, we stank like wet dogs.

At noon, having finished the men's bathroom, we knocked off for lunch. I went outside to get away from the dank toilets. The hotel was one of only a handful of structures in the area still standing upright—not half-collapsed or alarmingly slumped to one side—and another was a three-story building on the same block. A boxy blue car had appeared next to this building, and a tall man with black hair was looking through buckets of tools in the back. I was so tired, I didn't think much about it before walking over and introducing myself. Though I didn't know it then, Jun Akazaki had returned from Tokyo only a couple months before, after seeking shelter with his sister following the tsunami.

When I mentioned that my group had just finished work for the morning, he invited us over to his place for lunch. Later, when he told me about his café, I'd see this hospitality as part of his coffeehouse etiquette, but, at the time, I simply thought the gesture was typical of the kindness of the people of Tohoku—which, of course, it was.

I found Takeshi and told him about Jun's offer, and we toted our lunches of nori-wrapped rice balls next door. In a back room on the second floor, Jun was smoking Mild Sevens while his mother boiled water for coffee on a portable gas stove. Sitting on an overturned milk crate was a man with a shaved-bald head, whom Jun introduced as Watanabe-*san*; he seemed to be in his thirties, had come all the way from Hokkaido, and spoke very little. Jun and his mother had gotten folding chairs for the other Caritas volunteers, and I found another milk crate to sit on. The centerpiece of the makeshift dinette was a glass ashtray filled with cigarette butts and, behind me, "Doctor My Eyes" played on a small boom box. Jun had stripped the flooring out of the room and stretched blue tarps over the glassless windows.

"Are they going to rebuild here? Around the port?" I asked him.

"No new construction can go up for now," he said. "We'll have to see what the town decides. We might have to tear this place down at some point. We don't know yet."

Gutting the bathrooms, I'd pushed myself beyond thought and appetite, but talking with Jun, I came back to myself. In the morning, at the base camp, everyone had made tuna or salmon-filled *onigiri* with the rice left over from breakfast. In a minute flat, I devoured the two I'd packed.

Mrs. Akazaki handed cups of thin coffee around, and the wind snapped the edges of one of the tarps. I imagined what we looked like from high above, as we huddled in one of the few buildings left on the razed plain: around us excavators climbed on top of piles of rubble, dump trucks beeped while they backed through the half-destroyed city, and so much equipment moved about on what, from a God's-eye view, seemed to be an enormous construction site. I'd often done service work during my university days and had even been part of a trip that had built a makeshift schoolhouse in Juarez, Mexico—for it to be bulldozed only a couple weeks later. I knew, as a volunteer, you wanted to feel you were accomplishing something, but one person or group could do only so much. From above, we must've looked like ants crawling over a car crash, unable to understand the wreck, unaware of how incredibly beyond us it was.

July 20

The next morning, I got up later than I'd intended after a dreamless sleep. I'd been too tired to check my email the night before, so, with early light seeping in from around the edges of the curtain, I reached out of the futon's covers, turned on my computer, and logged onto the church's Wi-Fi. My mother's email was waiting:

Mike, Grandpa died early this morning. He woke up when Nan and I got there and knew who we were... He was comfortable and snoring and Nan fell asleep. At 5:30 a nurse woke her and told her he was gone. Actually, at 4:00 I had woken up and prayed that God would wrap my dad in comfort and take him to Heaven. So my prayers were answered. This has been so hard. He was such a good man...

It tore me up to see babies and young people there at Hospice that would never have the long life that Dad did. We are all kind of basket cases, but are supporting each other as best we can.

I know this is hard to get this news when you are working in a place where there has been so much loss of life and devastation. But Grandpa would want you to be doing the good work that you are doing. He was very proud of you.

Reading my mother's words, what was happening back in Ohio seemed to be in the air around me. I'd imagined when I heard the news, I'd feel a clear, sharp ache. I think I'd hoped the hurt would be proof of my love. I'd anticipated my grandfather's death though, and the thing forming in me was heavier than it was piercing, as though I'd drank a bucket of cement and it was hardening there in my belly, weighing me down. So, Grandpa was gone then.

I tried to draft a reply to my mom, but my words came out stolid and useless; I kept typing "sorry"—"I'm sorry to lose him," "Sorry I couldn't be there," "So sorry you have to go through this"—but none of what I wrote conveyed sorrow. I gave up and dragged myself to the morning meeting, but I heard little of what was said, and instead fell into a cycle of self-pity and then self-admonishment, guilt, and, once these had been exhausted, a simple, dull sadness.

Before long, the meeting broke up, and I got caught up in the morning routine. It felt good to run the vacuum, to pack a lunch, to load the van. To keep moving.

In Otsuchi, Takeshi, two newly arrived volunteers, and I continued gutting the hotel's second floor. The day before, when we'd returned from lunch, there had been a Toyota Prius parked in the lot across from the hotel, and a stocky man with uncombed hair had gotten out of it and come over, bowing and handing us both a copy of his business card as he shook our hands and apologized for not being there earlier in the morning. Kenichi Michimata's family had owned the Kotobuki Hotel for decades. His father's elderly second wife had been running it when the tsunami hit, and she'd been missing since the disaster, so the hotel was now his responsibility. However, he was a night school teacher in Morioka and couldn't come out to Otsuchi every day. Kenichi had asked us to tear out anything that wasn't concrete before we did any more pressure washing, and so Takeshi and I spent the morning ripping down the tile ceilings on the second floor.

At noon, we went again to the Akazaki's for lunch with Jun, his mother, and Watanabe. This time, Jun had a Beatles compilation on the CD player, and I talked with him about classic rock and Japanese folk music from the sixties and seventies, which I'd learned about from one of my professors in college. Of course, I realized Jun must have still been grieving the tsunami, and I wanted to commiserate with him about my grandfather, but I held back. I didn't ask him to tell me about his loss. I imagined he'd been offered so many expressions of condolence he probably felt the only part of him people saw was his grief. I figured he'd had his fill of other people's pity.

We fell into a silence, listening to an excavator digging through the rubble, until Takeshi asked if the area around the hotel had been near the center of town before the waves came.

Jun nodded toward the street in front of his building: "Across there, the burned building was a grocery. Next to the hotel was a shoe store."

"Does the mayor have a plan?" I asked.

"The mayor died in the tsunami, so nothing's decided. There has to be a vote, but everyone is spread out. In refugee shelters, in the temporary housing, with relatives, all over the country," he said. As I'd later learn, most the local officials had been at the town hall when the earthquake struck—only the deputy mayor and twenty others, whom the mayor sent to the roof, had survived. "It wasn't a big town, but sometimes jazz acts or bands from Sendai would come up."

Mrs. Akazaki handed me a cup of coffee, and I was glad for its warmth in my hands. In Tohoku, along the Sanriku Coast, the rainy season that summer stretched from mid-June well into July, and, to me, it seemed it was cloudy more days than not in Otsuchi. I figured Jun was in his early fifties, which would've made him roughly the same age as Uncle Russ, my mom's younger brother. There were other similarities: they were both middle-aged bachelors, and, with my grandfather gone, my uncle and grandmother would have only each other, much like Jun and his mother. I had no doubt Jun felt the same way about Otsuchi as Russ did about Willowick, his hometown. My grandparents had moved there after Grandpa returned from the War, part of a wave of Eastern Europeans who migrated to East Lake in the forties. By the time my mom began bringing me there, those Slovenian, Polish, and Croatian neighbors were in their golden years, and a thick, retirement-community quiet had settled over the area. It made me restless, but, for Russ, the hushed air and the smell of grilling brats in the summer was home.

Surely, Otsuchi had held its own tranquil charm. I imagined dim bars and ramen restaurants smelling of long-simmering pork broth, old fishing boats rusting in the harbor. These were my memories of Mutsu, and, through my memories of that place, I could understand some sliver of Jun's affection for his hometown—as well as his pain at its ruin.

After we returned to the base, I soaked my limbs in the bathhouse, and, before the evening meeting, I called Junko. When I told her about my grandfather, I didn't break down and she gave me all the appropriate words of sympathy. Somehow, when we talked about my grandfather, whom she'd never met, or when I asked her about her father's health, which was steadily diminishing, our conversation became distant. Though our upbringings had been very different, we'd both been raised with a sense of emotional restraint. Loss meant a turn inward. To do otherwise, to cry in public or grieve in front of others, was a kind of vulgarity; the experiences and memories that led us to feel loss were, after all, ours alone.

Demolishing the walls in the hotel had exhausted me, and the bath's hot water had leached out the rest of my strength. If I closed my eyes, I could almost feel her next to me in the warm pocket between the futon pad and a set of heavy covers.

I said, "I miss sleeping next to you."

She told me she missed it too. Still, I had to get up and drag myself across the hall to the evening meeting in the women's dorm, so Junko and I said our goodbyes. Takeshi gave a report about what we'd done at the hotel, and, for the most part, I was able to remain silent and let my attention weave through and around what was being said, as though the clusters of words were clouds I could pass in and out of.

During the meeting, my eyes kept returning to Ise, the base's quiet leader. Other than a few exchanges in the halls, we hadn't talked much since I'd arrived. I'd heard her speak up only once to remind the volunteers to empathize with how much the survivors had lost, to respect the privacy of their suffering. I sensed the experience behind her tone. After all, her home had been through a catastrophe, and I was sure she'd known many of those who were now missing. But then again, this was true of almost everyone I'd met in the disaster area. For Jun, it was the old man next door, who'd turned down the offer of a ride to the evacuation area and been lost to the waves.

Normally, Jun would have attended a wake and memorial in honor of his neighbor. But so many were dead, so many still missing. Most survivors had seen something or someone they loved washed away, and anyone you met in the disaster area likely had bitter memories. Whatever impulse there was to share suffering was trumped by the need to get through the day, the week—maybe next month those feelings could be dealt with, maybe next year.

Certainly, I could understand the impulse to keep to oneself, but this stoicism had a dark side. Ryokan Ogayu, the Buddhist priests whom Jun had helped pull from the wreckage, had lost his father and eldest son to the waves. Three months after the disaster, his second daughter, who worked as a kindergarten teacher in Tokyo, killed herself in her apartment. She left behind a note, saying: *I'm going to meet Grandpa and Older Brother.* Overwhelmed, Ryokan shut himself inside his temporary housing unit and spent day after day drinking sake.

Many people in the disaster area were struggling to deal with what they'd been through. In my own way, I was also looking for an outlet, but

I wasn't going to inflict my grief on people like Jun and Ise, who'd already lost so much.

This was why, when, before the closing prayer, Sister Ozawa announced that a morning Mass would be held in a few days, I resolved to go. In the back of my mind was Graham Greene's conversion, and I remembered something he'd written, a memory he'd given one of his characters, that spoke to the sensual nature of the Catholic service: "...the white muslin dresses—he remembered the smell of incense in the churches of his boyhood, the candles and the laciness." I thought the ritual might help me sort through my feelings, and, though a single Mass wasn't going to bring me to religion, it might point me in the right direction.

July 23

I woke later than I'd meant to and quietly hurried out of the men's dorm. In the gravel lot outside, I walked over the stepping-stones to the church and cast my eyes up at the hills where ribbons of white fog rose from the valley between the dark green slopes.

The sanctuary was on the second floor, and, as I took the stairs, I heard a hymn finishing up. A heavy sliding door was closed over the entrance, and, putting my eye to the gap between the two wooden panels, I saw the congregation standing before the priest, who stood behind a stone altar in a white robe, candles flanking him and his head bowed while he recited a prayer.

I had heard from one of the long-term volunteers that, before taking his vows, he'd been in the Naval Self-Defense Forces. Father Toru was tall and kept his head clean shaven, and, with his clipped speech, stiff posture, and shy laughter, he always seemed to be ready for his commanding officer to storm into the room.

I waited until he finished, and then slid one of the door panels aside. Everyone turned at the rumble, but I didn't meet their eyes and slunk into a pew near the back. It was the first Mass I could remember attending. Between the readings, I joined in singing the Psalm, and I tried to keep up with the liturgy but was soon lost by the translation of the Bible. As I moved my eyes over the yellow- and red-colored glass of the church's windows and looked at the starved and bloody Jesus figurine that hung on the cross behind the altar, I thought of my grandfather, forcing myself to imagine what he'd experienced in his last moments. There was the torturous anxiety I felt whenever I thought of death but also a sense of calm: he'd lived a full life. I was relieved when, near the end of the service, I could kneel down with the rest of the congregation to pray.

After the Lord's Prayer, Father Toru began preparing the Eucharist. I didn't know the rules about who could take communion but decided I would receive it if offered. After the rest of the congregation had gone forward, I walked down the aisle and stood before the altar. The Father asked if I'd been confirmed—at first, I thought he wanted to know if I'd been baptized and said yes, then I realized he'd used a different word and said no. Flustered, he held out a wafer.

I took the offering and placed it on my tongue, selected a plastic cup of watery wine from the silver tray, and tipped it back—already beginning to realize I was still nowhere near faith or even the first step toward it. The other volunteers at the Mass were so quiet and solemn, and their seriousness hinted at their belief. As with the church I'd gone to in Ohio, I'd hoped that, by being around the faithful, I might find my own way into their conviction. But, by the time I filed out of the church with the others, I saw no matter how I tried, I couldn't to make myself believe that the pale wafer was the transubstantiated body of Christ. Nor would I ever think the wine was His blood. And, though I believed in Jesus as a historical figure, when he became the Son of God, set above all other people, he was lost to me. Looking back, I see how my own flaws had sabotaged me: I'd gone looking for faith, armed only with doubt. I couldn't change who I was so easily, though, in many other ways, my approach to the world—believing in what I saw around me every day: the beauty of nature, the goodness of people, the damage each of us carries—had served me well. I wanted to believe in something more expansive and rigorous, but, after the Mass, I was no closer to finding it.

So, as I filed out of the sanctuary with the others, I felt only a sense of calm and perhaps a bit more focus. I hadn't experienced a revelation, but I had moved forward in my mourning for Grandpa. I'd loved him and would still continue to grieve him; I was one step further along.

That morning, Takeshi let me drive to the hotel so I could learn the roads. When we got back to the base camp later in the evening, he would pack his things and get ready to go home to Sendai the next morning; I still had my Japanese driver's license from when I'd lived in Mutsu, and, since I was the only volunteer who'd worked at the hotel and would still be around after he left, the driving duties would fall to me.

In Otsuchi, the local Council of Social Welfare—which, like Caritas in Kamaishi, was organizing the people who were coming from all over the country to help with the recovery in Tohoku—had sent seven volunteers to the hotel. In addition, when we arrived, three women from Morioka, who knew Kenichi Michimata, were already cleaning the rooms on the third and fourth floors of the hotel. Takeshi and I showed the Social Welfare volunteers the progress we'd made in gutting the first two floors and then broke into two teams.

The young man and two young women who'd ended up with me seemed to be college-aged, though, once we started working, it was too loud to ask them. I'd figured out a method for demolishing the dropped ceilings on the first floor that involved me standing on a short stepladder and swinging the giant wooden hammer, bringing entire sections of mud-encrusted tile crashing down. The Social Welfare volunteers would scoop the rubble into a wheelbarrow and dump it outside, where a pile of debris had formed next to the hotel.

Around noon, Takeshi and I joined the women from Morioka on the hotel's roof to eat the lunches we'd brought. It was a Saturday, and Jun Akazaki and his mother had taken the day off from working on their building, and the Social Welfare volunteers had returned to their center for lunch. After we finished eating and the Social Welfare volunteers returned, the three women from Morioka got in their car and we saw them off as they started the two-hour drive back.

Going back inside, I climbed up on my ladder and resumed demolishing the ceiling. I was taking a break when I felt trembling under my feet that built into a quake. The world blurred as vibrations shook through the walls, the ceiling, and even my body. I hadn't heard the shaking coming, but, as the tremors stopped, a quiet settled over the ruined coast. Though the quake had been fairly long, I was still surprised when Takeshi called out.

"Are you okay?" he asked.

"We're fine," I answered.

He came hurrying down from the second floor. "Should we go?"

"Where?" I asked.

"Evacuate."

I hesitated, reluctant to leave. In the four days I'd worked at the hotel, we'd never had so many volunteers. In one morning, we'd gotten more done than in the past two days.

The other volunteers filtered downstairs as the squeal of a tsunami siren rose into the air. I looked out the window; a police car was racing up the road, blasting a garbled announcement over its speakers. I couldn't make out the words, but I knew we had to go. Right now.

Takeshi and I piled into the Caritas van, and the older man who'd come with volunteers from the Council of Social Welfare got behind the wheel of their car. We pulled out onto the road, Takeshi driving toward the small mountain in the middle of the town—the same rise where Jun and his mother had taken shelter the day of the tsunami. The siren cried out again. Near the mountain, the traffic slowed to a crawl, and I looked back to make sure the Social Welfare volunteers' car was still behind us. I dug my phone out of my work gear, but, when I looked at the screen, I saw there was no signal.

Takeshi inched forward, following the car ahead of us up the road to the community center nestled in the foothills of the mountain. When we finally crested the first hill, the community center's parking lot was full, so Takeshi pulled over onto the shoulder of the road. The sense of urgency was fading as the Social Welfare volunteers pulled up behind us.

We got out of our vehicles, Takeshi took a small group to use the bathrooms, and the rest of the volunteers and I wandered the flat area around the community center, killing time until the all clear was announced and we could return to the hotel. I had been to the Shiroyama Community Center a couple of times and had looked inside the gymnasium, where dozens of refugees were still living while they waited to be assigned to temporary housing units. I went to the knee-high guardrail, which ringed the drive that encircled the community center. Beyond the metal barrier, the slope fell sharply down. From there, the part of town that I could see had all been devastated by the tsunami. Beyond the corpses of buildings was the terrible ocean. Blue, blue, and more blue.

Looking out on what remained, I felt my sense of sadness for my grandfather beginning to release. Like the flattened landscape before me, loss was something to mourn, but, eventually, the ruined edifices of grief had to be torn down and buried so that new constructions could be erected. For those who were left behind, life was still there, waiting.

In a way, this was what I had attempted to write in my contribution to my grandfather's eulogy, when I'd emailed my mother the day before. I'd talked with her over Skype, and she'd told me about the memorial service she was planning, which would be held at Shoregate United Methodist, a few blocks from her childhood home. She'd made a PowerPoint and put together a display of his ham radio QSL cards and Purple Heart, and she asked me to write something for the pastor to be read at the service. In the couple of paragraphs I'd come up with, I tried to capture the importance of making peace with the ones we've lost, so that they might rest and we might move forward into the world that had been left to us.

I rewrote my contribution several times. It was simple and sentimental, but I also hoped it was enough:

When I met my grandfather, he'd already accomplished the achievements that defined his life—he'd fought in the Second World War, married my grandmother, worked at Bailey Meter for more than forty years, and raised three children, including my mother, Marjorie... He loved life, and taught me to enjoy the simple, the everyday. I remember driving out to the country in the Crown Vic with him, searching between the farmers' fields for the vegetable stand that sold the sweet, pale yellow corn he liked—looking for the ear that was just the right size, with a husk the right shade of green. And I remember his knowing smile when we found what he wanted, a smile that assured me we'd carry it back in the car, and eat it at the dinner table with Russ and Grandma, and then all sleep under the same roof together.

I, along with the rest of my family and everyone who ever knew him, have suffered a great loss. But, while his death is sad, my grandfather's life is something to be celebrated. Having enjoyed the long and beautiful journey, may his soul rest in peace.

II. The Dream People's Café

Otsuchi Town, Iwate Prefecture

At first, Jun Akazaki didn't feel like fixing anything at all. The building he and his mother had lived in for decades had been flooded up to the second story; the waves had filled it with mud, rubble, and the garbage that had formerly been their prized possessions.

After passing the night of the disaster in the gymnasium of the Shiroyama Community Center along with a swollen crowd of refugees, he and his mother had begun moving from place to place. They'd gotten a ride with a friend to the house of a farmer, where they stayed a couple days before moving on to the sports park in the town's Terano District, which had space for them to sleep on the hardwood floor of the archery range; they made their beds on cardboard and plastic sheeting, a stone's throw from the baseball stadium and the indoor basketball courts, where bodies recovered from the wreckage were being laid out. Finally, Jun's cousin came to get them. Satomi was about his age, married, with two children, and her family of four lived with her grandparents in a two-story house in the Sakuragi District. The first floor of their home had been inundated, and her grandparents had taken refuge inland after the tsunami. Jun and his mother managed to squeeze into the second floor with the rest of Satomi's family. Anyway, it was better than sleeping with strangers in the sports park.

On day six of the aftermath, Jun went to look at his building. The roads were gone, buried under debris, and walking through the rubble was slow going. Around him, Self-Defense Force soldiers in green-camo uniforms moved in squads through the ruins, searching for the deceased, pulling drowned and lifeless bodies from piles of boards and sections of roofs. As he climbed through the wreckage, Jun saw several corpses that the soldiers hadn't yet reached. The town was as series of craters, as if he was walking through the outcome of a bombing campaign.

As the tsunami had thrust inland, it'd picked up dirt, churning the earth into waves so that it coated everything it touched with a layer of mud. Reeking, black sludge was everywhere, but, as Jun neared his building, the smell of acrid charcoal filled his nose.

When he came around the base of the Shiroyama foothills, he was relieved to see his building was standing and hadn't been touched by the fires that had raged through the Honcho and Omachi districts. The flooding had nearly reached the third floor, and the windows on the first two floors were busted out. He hoped the valuables they kept upstairs were safe.

After this initial visit, the next time Jun returned to his building was with his mother, when his brother-in-law, Masato, drove up in his van. With six of them living in the one undamaged floor of Satomi's house, they were cramped, and everything was stretched thin. Jun's sister, Megumi, insisted they come stay with her in Tokyo and sent her husband up to get them. By then, the Self-Defense Forces had cleared the main roads, and they were able to drive over to the building. Masato and Jun carried down the three new TV sets they'd kept stored on the third floor, his mother's old kimonos, and her jewelry. From there, it was a seven-hour drive down to Tokyo.

Ten days, Jun and his mother stayed with Masato, Megumi, and their son in Koto Ward, in eastern Tokyo. For Jun's nephew, a third-grade elementary school student, the tsunami was an impossibility he couldn't quite wrap his mind around, but Megumi had so many questions for Jun. He did his best to answer, though there was much he didn't know; once the quake hit, he'd been cut off from information, and much of what he'd heard was based on rumor and speculation. When he needed air, Jun walked the streets around her house. Nearby was a big park, with tennis courts and barbecue grills, a paved track for people to walk their dogs, and a green where pairs of kids kicked soccer balls back and forth. The surrounding neighborhoods were a mix of high-rise apartments, small factories, and old lumber warehouses that were gradually disappearing and being replaced by coffee shops, restaurants, and art galleries.

But no matter how pleasant the area was, it would never be Jun's home. When he'd left Otsuchi, he'd left his life behind. From Tokyo, it was hard to figure out what was going on back in his hometown. He got in touch with his brother, Takuya, who lived in Ofunato, south of Otsuchi; Jun asked if he could come stay with him and his wife in their apartment in the hills above the bay, well out of the waves' reach. When Masato offered to help buy a used car that he could drive up to Iwate, he was humbled by the generosity.

Upon returning to Otsuchi at the end of March, Jun was deflated by what he saw. His building was structurally sound—his father had built it strong, with reinforced-concrete—but it was still the same mess he'd seen before he left.

Mud and debris packed the first floor. Some things he recognized as having belonged to him and his mother before the disaster, but others he had no idea where they'd come from. He didn't feel like cleaning out the garbage, and instead checked to see which of their valuables had survived undamaged and looked in on his friends. Search and rescue teams were still going through the neighboring buildings, spray painting the structures they'd checked to mark that they were clear of human remains.

About a month after he came back from Tokyo, his mother came to stay with Jun's brother as well. Takuya taught Japanese history at Ofunato High School, and his wife was also a teacher. The two of them had to be at their schools during the day, and Jun and his mother would make the hour-long drive to Otsuchi.

When Jun's mother saw the half-destroyed hillside cemetery, she'd asked, "Can't we clean this up a little?"

Jun started with the graves on the lower levels of the temple, where his family plot was. Each of the stone plots had a receptacle in the back to hold the tall boards painted with names and death dates of the loved ones interred there. He searched for theses markers in the tsunami muck and washed off the ones he found.

Toward the end of April, he went to a relief event where volunteers were giving out plates of hot food to survivors, and a friend of Jun's introduced him to a volunteer who'd come all the way down from Hokkaido by himself. A couple days after meeting Jun, this man showed up at the ruins of the cemetery, introducing himself in as few words as he could manage: "Hello, I'm Toshinori Watanabe." They'd started working together, looking through the rubble for the boards from the grave markers, washing them, sorting them by family.

It was slow going, but Toshinori was careful in everything he did. He barely talked as they wiped down the planks of wood with dirty rags, though, as April turned to May, Jun began to piece together bits of his story. He was from Fukui Prefecture but had been living in Asahikawa before the disaster. As a child, he'd hated school, skipping out on much of his secondary education, though, later, he'd traveled to Europe and lived in Belgium, where he spent three years learning woodworking. He'd also spent part of his youth hitchhiking across Japan, including Iwate Prefecture, with nothing but a wheelbarrow to carry his things in. He'd been moved by the images of the disaster and came down in a van to do what he could to help. But he wasn't the type to join one of the big volunteer organizations; no, he was sleeping in his car, parking wherever he could find a space at night, preferably near a bathroom and running water.

By the time I arrived in July, he'd been working with the Akazaki's for almost three months. He had a back-to-the-land aspect about him that fascinated me; he could seem naïve at times and incredibly profound at others. One day, when we were sitting, having coffee with Jun and his mother, I saw a car outside on the road and watched a man and woman get out to take pictures of the beached fishing trawlers and burned-out neighborhoods. I muttered an off-hand complaint about the disaster tourists. I wanted to see myself as different; I was there to help, not to gawk at the ruins.

But Toshinori said, "They're not so bad. It's good just to come see, to look with your own eyes, that's better than seeing it on TV. You feel it in a different way. It becomes real."

Of course, he was right, and the suddenness of this insight swept all the other half-formed thoughts in my head.

By this time, he and Jun were working to get the Akazaki's building ready to use again. The town needed a place for people to get together—Jun's middle-aged friends, but also his mother's haiku circle—a place where anyone who wanted to could come enjoy a cup of coffee, a few minutes of conversation. Toshinori put his woodworking skills to use, covering the rough, damaged parts of the interior walls with bits of siding. The second floor had suffered less than the first, and, Jun figured, with a few months' work they could use the space to reopen Mumins, the name his mother had given the café after a Finnish cartoon show. To spell the name, she'd picked out Chinese characters that matched the foreign sounds. When you put them together, the characters meant something like "space-dream people."

Jun's dream was to get his old band back together, to use his café to put on shows for the local survivors and bring together the other musicians in the area. As for Toshinori, he'd told me he wanted to start a store when he went back to Hokkaido. When I asked what kind of store, he said he didn't want to sell anything in particular: "I just want it to be a place where people can come to communicate with one another. Communication, that's the important thing."

I nodded at this, though I had no idea what he meant. Still, I could understand why someone who struggled to say much about himself or what he thought would be interested in communication; he wasn't a quiet man because he had nothing to say, but because as soon as he started to speak, he entered into a complicated series of relations that could spin off in any direction at all.

Of course, the complexity of language mirrors the complexity of society, but, in the first months after the tsunami, life in the disaster zone was drastically simplified. Money was of little use and typical ideas of work condensed, as everyone became employed in some version of repairing the town. But, gradually, as the summer grew late, the mood in Otsuchi was changing. A Lawson's convenience store went up a few minutes down the road from the Akazaki's building, and then a series of big-box clothing and home-improvement stores reopened in a nearby mall. The police were no longer occupied with searching the ruins and resumed their regular patrols. Gradually, the city was drawing up plans and cracking down on unauthorized land use.

This was all part of the town getting back on its feet, but it also signaled the end of a sense of possibility. Soon, the survivors and refugees would all be moved into temporary housing units, and the authorities might begin giving Toshinori trouble about where he parked his car to sleep at night. They might wonder where he was employed, or what organization he was with—all conversations he'd probably rather avoid.

After working with him for a couple months, Jun noticed Toshinori had started meeting up with a young woman from the town after he finished work. One day, out of the blue, Toshinori said, "I think she and I will get married." Sure enough, once he'd helped Jun reopen his café in October, Toshinori packed his and the woman's things in his car, and they started the drive back to Hokkaido together.

III. The Base Camp

Otsuchi Town, Iwate Prefecture

Of all the people I met during the recovery, Kenichi Michimata, the willful owner of the Kotobuki Hotel, made one of the strongest impressions on me; and perhaps it was because of his uncompromising nature that the following years followed wound up being so hard on him.

But I didn't really start to get to know Kenichi until after Takeshi left.

On a chilly Sunday morning, the other volunteers and I gathered outside the church, where Hiramatsu was loading suitcases and duffel bags into an idling van. Takeshi and the others were saying their goodbyes, exchanging contact information and promises to send pictures to the people they'd met; a veteran volunteer named Tanizawa would drive them to Kamaishi Station. I went to Takeshi and was about to bow, but he held out his hand. When I took it, he tightened his grip and said, "Thank you"—the only words I'd ever heard him speak in English. Not one to prolong things, he quickly handed me his business card and then ducked into the van. I stood with the other volunteers, waving while they pulled out of the drive, a little numb at his leaving.

Takeshi had been with me at the hotel from the start, and I was unsure about working without him. He'd been good at explaining what we were doing to the volunteers who worked with us for only a day to two, and, though I couldn't put it into words, I think I recognized how his calm balanced my more reckless nature. With him gone, I'd have to drive the Caritas van to the hotel, orient anyone who signed up to work there, and help them stay safe.

This last part would be a tricky, as the hotel was littered with broken boards and twisted metal. In the interest of getting as much done as possible during my time as a volunteer, I'd adopted a few techniques in violation of the Caritas' safety guidelines, such as standing on a ladder and swinging a giant wooden hammer to demolish the drop-tile ceilings. I figured, if you wanted to accomplish something, you couldn't waste time following each little rule.

Taking these risks had earned me a few cuts and bruises, but, despite my ill-advised methods, the worst I'd gotten was a nail through the bottom of my boot. I'd been demolishing a wall with a crowbar when I stepped on a board on the edge of a rubble pile. Out of breath, I hadn't seen the rusty spike sticking out of it, but I felt the nail stab me. I hobbled away—instantly recovering my senses—and sat down on the floor and took off my boot. Peeling off my sweaty sock, I saw a deep pink scratch on my wet, raisin-like flesh, but no blood. The nail hadn't broken the skin. I didn't tell anyone, but, for a few days after, I racked my brain trying to remember when my last tetanus booster had been. In idle moments I opened and closed my mouth, trying to recall everything I knew about lockjaw. I also began to long for a pair of the heavy-duty boots that I'd seen professional construction workers wearing.

But the pay from my teaching in grad school wasn't much. I'd spent all my money getting to Japan and had worked on a garlic farm to earn some cash for expenses, but even that was almost gone. I had no idea how I was going to pay my train fair after I finished volunteering, let alone how I could afford a pair of steel-reinforced boots that I was going to use for only a week.

So, after seeing Takeshi off, I picked out the sturdiest pair of rubber boots from the collection at the base camp, which any volunteer was free to use, before heading out. I also made sure to grab a dust mask and fill one of the five-liter jugs from the camp with ice water. The mask kept me from inhaling the grit thrown up during demolition and would invariably be filthy by midday, and I'd wind up drinking all the water before I left. It was hard, thirsty work, and often I found myself soaked in sweat after the first hour. Not long after my grandfather's death, my exhaustion had begun to catch up with me. At night, I'd lie down, feeling the soreness in every part of my body until my consciousness was overcome by a black sleep so thick, no fragment of my dreams, which were usually so vivid, ever escaped.

In spite of these difficulties, I was glad to be handed sole leadership of the hotel project. It was different from the work I did in grad school, which revolved around books, my students' papers, days sitting in classrooms, and evenings spent staring at the screen of my laptop. What I did in Otsuchi was so much more tangible: when I arrived in the morning, there was a wall, and when I left in the afternoon, it was gone. I also enjoyed the sense of camaraderie I felt with the others. Though we mostly talked about tools and the best way to rip out different kinds of interior paneling, doing manual labor alongside the rest of the volunteers helped me bond with them in ways that, as a foreigner, might have otherwise been impossible for me; when we were shoveling or hammering together, our differences seemed to melt away.

I wanted to keep working at the hotel, though I was afraid I might make some mistake. Word that I'd disregarded one of the safety-first rules would get back to the base camp, and, like that, I'd be taken off the project.

The day before, I'd heard the group of volunteers who'd come from the local Council of Social Welfare say they'd be at the hotel again on Sunday, and, because it was the weekend, Kenichi didn't have to work at the night school in Morioka where he taught. It would take him a couple hours to drive out though, and he wouldn't be there until later in the afternoon. Altogether, there would be a lot of bodies to keep track of.

This was why, the day after Takeshi left, I was nervous as I piloted the light truck out to Otsuchi alone. Indulging myself, I turned on the heater while rolling down the window a crack. I tuned the radio until I found a rock station and cranked it up.

At the hotel, I assessed the headway Takeshi and I had made; the second floor was gutted, ready to be pressure washed. Kenichi had said he hoped to start using the hotel to host volunteers in August. If I was going to help him meet that goal, I needed to get started on the first floor, which was bigger and which the waves had slammed even harder, pushing over a wooden wall in the back that hadn't been part of the original structure.

Despite how much I wanted to make progress, when the Social Welfare volunteers did show up, I tried to stick to the rules and kept them on the least dangerous tasks: scooping up the last of the rubble on the second floor, ripping out doorjambs. At noon, Tanizawa came and watched me shovel debris into a wheelbarrow, occasionally squatting down in his spotless purple jeans to sweep grit into a dustpan.

Tanizawa wasn't much help in terms of work, but I enjoyed listening to him. Aside from Ise, Hiramatsu, and the other staff members, he was one of the longest-serving volunteers at the base camp. He usually worked alone, and his main project was a free taxi service for elderly refugees in the Shiroyama Community Center. Many of these senior citizens needed to go to the hospital for regular checkups or to the drug store to refill their medications, but they couldn't walk up and down the steep hill to the community center. So Tanizawa set up a schedule where he'd pick up passengers on the top of the hill and drive them wherever they needed to go. Most of his regulars finished their trips into town by early afternoon, and he'd often turn up at the hotel to lend a hand and talk. He was from the Kansai region, western Japan, and was a natural storyteller. At the evening meetings, his reports could go on for a quarter hour or more, veering between his reflections, jokes, and anecdotes about the people he'd driven.

As I shoveled debris into a wheelbarrow, he told me about Kobe after the Great Hanshin Earthquake. He'd worked in a bar in the city, and, after the disaster, he said the worst thing had been the sense of isolation. The highways going into Kobe were impassible, no trains were running, and, meanwhile, people were still buried under the rubble.

"This time, after the disaster people complained about survivors getting drunk while everything was ruined," he said. "In a situation like that, you may as well drink what you got."

I smiled. There were strict rules at base camp against volunteers drinking, but I got the sense Tanizawa would've enjoyed relaxing with a cold beer or two in the evening; I would've been glad to join him for that matter. I hefted my wheelbarrow, pushed it outside, and dumped it on the rubble pile, which was taller than I was by then.

Not long after Tanizawa left, Kenichi arrived in his Prius. Unlike the first day we'd met, when he'd worn a button down and dark slacks, he was in new pair of work pants and a light gray jacket. We bowed and shook hands again. I showed him the progress we'd made and what was left to do. I'd eventually learn how hardworking of a man Kenichi was, how impatient he was to realize his intentions; on our first day together, he insisted we start ripping down the ceilings on the first floor.

The Social Welfare volunteers were cleaning up for the day, but I had a few hours before I needed to go back, so I set up my ladder and climbed up with the wooden mallet to show him my method. The trick was to aim for the aluminum supports that held up the ceiling tiles. When the hammer's head caught one of these metal strips and tore it out, the result was a tremendous crashing, as loose tiles fell through the air and shattered against the floor. But using both hands to swing the hammer meant I couldn't hold onto the ladder, and, if I missed—if the hammer's head failed to hit anything—the momentum could send me flying into the air like a cartoon character running into the emptiness beyond an animated cliff's edge. This was compounded by the fact that, although I took a hard hat with me every day, for the most part I'd stopped wearing it because the foam cushions inside absorbed my sweat until they were soaked like sponges; whenever I adjusted the helmet, the cushions would send cold rivulets of perspiration running down my face. Instead, I tied a towel around my head and took it off several times a day to ring it out.

As I demonstrated my technique, Kenichi held the ladder, and when I glanced down, he was looking at me from under the brim of his own hard hat, beaming at the speed with which I worked. He disappeared for a moment and came back with a step stool and a crowbar; he set up in the corner opposite me and began tearing down the ceiling from that side. Though I had a full-sized ladder and worked standing two or three rungs below the top, Kenichi had to stand on the third and top step of his stool. We'd been working like this for an hour or so, pausing only to climb down and move our ladders, when the Social Welfare volunteers came back.

The Council of Social Welfare wasn't affiliated with any religion or political party—it was just a local non-profit organization helping to coordinate volunteers who came to Iwate—but in the two days I'd worked with this particular group of volunteers, I'd gotten the impression they'd come to Otsuchi together, as part of the same organization. This wasn't unusual, as many high schools and community groups were planning service trips to help with the recovery effort.

When this group of Social Welfare volunteers returned, they were in a sleek-looking coach bus. Two young women who we'd worked with earlier in the day walked into the hotel. One went toward Kenichi, and a girl who'd volunteered with Takeshi and me came in my direction.

She said hi before asking, "Will you accept my prayers?"

Not wanting to offend, I said, "Sure."

I thought this would be goodbye—that she would return to the bus and pray for me in the privacy of her own thoughts. Instead, she took both my hands in hers and, holding them between us, bowed her head and began to speak: "Dear gods..."

I bowed my head in imitation of her and tried to listen but could only pick out phrases here and there: "Protect this person from harm... keep his heart warm." Out of the corner of my eye, I looked at Kenichi, who also stood with his head bowed, though he'd had the sense to press his palms together in the Christian attitude of supplication. Too late, I realized I should've done this rather than let the girl take my hands, which were going clammy in her grip.

She finished her prayer and let go, and I wiped my sweaty palms on my windbreaker. We exchanged bows again, and she and the other volunteer hurried out and got on their bus.

Kenichi and I wandered outside to see them off. We waved at the bus's tinted windows as it pulled away, and, still in a strange, mild shock, I asked, "What was that?" I'd heard Buddhist prayers before and knew they didn't sound like what the girl had said. "Were they some kind of Christian?"

"A sort of Shinto, I think," Kenichi said.

I knew there were many esoteric sects of Buddhism and Shinto, an indigenous system of animistic beliefs. Most often, spirituality is a personal matter in Japan—not something people talk about in public—and I hadn't thought to ask about their religion while we were working together. However, perhaps it was because of these prayers that I later asked Kenichi about his beliefs. He was Catholic, and he would tell me about how he'd decided to convert when he was a lost young man, working odd jobs, unsure of what he wanted. He'd happened upon a book called *Life of Jesus* by Shusaku Endo, the great Catholic novelist. The experience of the book and the depictions of Jesus' suffering had affected him profoundly, and, not long after, he'd gone to the Catholic Church in Kamaishi and asked to be baptized. By the time I met him, he was decades into his faith, but, like Tanizawa, who was a parishioner at a church in Kobe, Kenichi had an imprudent character; he could become totally absorbed by his aims, to the point that he became the very embodiment of intent, moving straight through any obstacle between him and his goals. His motivations were as complex as anyone's, but when he was working, he thought only of work. When he drove, he didn't listen to the radio or play with the heater; he simply steered his car directly toward his destination.

So, although the Social Welfare volunteers' prayers had left us both a little stunned, Kenichi wasn't to be deterred. We didn't talk about the oddness of what had happened as we turned back inside.

A few minutes later, I was taking a break, considering a piece of a wall I'd eventually need to rip out, when I heard a high scream. I looked to see Kenichi in midair—the toothpaste white of his hard hat and the light gray of his work clothes stood out against the concrete—falling so his helmet and shoulder hit the ground at the same time. He crumpled into a heap. His crowbar rang against the floor. Already my legs were carrying me toward him.

He was a heavy man, but he still had strength in his legs, and I was able to help him up. He sat on his stool, which had somehow stayed upright. He clenched his teeth and panted but didn't cry out.

I kept asking, "Are you— you okay?"

"It just hurts a little."

He moved his upper body around, trying to feel for any pain. He was able to roll his arm in a circle, but, at the top of the arc, he squeezed his eyes shut in agony.

"Feel here." He pointed to where his neck and shoulder met.

At first, I touched him through his clothes, but I couldn't feel anything. I pulled his collar aside and worked my hand inside his shirt, feeling the warm skin above his collarbone. I had no idea what I should be feeling for, so I put my other hand to my own neck and shoulder for comparison. I pushed away the strange, sudden feeling of intimacy that came with touching a man whose body I hadn't given a second thought to until just a moment before. I shook this thought off—I didn't need to be wandering off into my own musing right then.

"It feels normal," I said. "Maybe a bit swollen. Nothing out of place."

"I was surprised," he said. And then, grinning, "That girl must've put a curse on me."

I laughed with him, realizing how fast my heart was going. He was okay, I said to myself, forcing the thought through my mind; the fall had looked bad, but he was okay. After a few minutes, we went back to work, but Kenichi's shoulder was still aching, and I needed to start heading back to the base in Kamaishi anyway. Within half an hour, we called it quits.

Kenichi took his hard hat off and went upstairs to put his crowbar and step stool with the collection of tools he kept on the second floor.

He came back down and walked out of the hotel toward his car, and I followed him, calling his name.

A few days before, while tearing down the ceilings on the second floor, I'd seen a kind of small box come crashing down with the tiles. When I climbed down and picked it up, I realized it was a photo book, filled with pictures of a younger Kenichi: him on a white-sand beach, him standing in a dense jungle, him holding a plate of food at a luau, where he wore a floral shirt and tiki torches burned in the background. It must've been an album from a vacation he'd taken to Hawai'i or Guam. It had been stored in the ceiling tiles on the second floor, which had been just high enough to keep it out of the tsunami waters. The photos themselves hadn't suffered any damage, and I thought he'd be happy to see them again.

Yet, when I took the album to him in the parking lot, he opened it, glanced at a few pages, and grunted to himself. He thanked me in a perfunctory way, set the album on the curb in front of his white Prius, and began taking off his windbreaker, wincing at the effort it took to get his arms out of the sleeves. He was sore and tired, I reasoned, turning back to the hotel. In a few days, after some rest, he'd feel better and be glad to look through the old photos.

I was exhausted myself. The work and the fright of Kenichi's fall had drained me. So, on the drive home, instead of taking the bypass, which led through several tunnels under the mountains, I followed the older prefectural highway along the coast; I took my time getting back to Kamaishi, and, when I arrived, the day's light was fading. I pulled into the church's driveway and was unloading the van when Ise came outside.

"I got a call from Michimata-*san*," she said. "What happened today?"

I felt myself go red as I explained Kenichi's fall. "But he was okay," I stammered. "He'd kept working and then got in his car and drove himself home."

Ise said, "He went by a doctor on his way. He broke his collarbone."

My stomach rolled over. When I saw Kenichi next, he'd tell me how the doctor said he'd been in shock. Regardless, I could see how this looked to Ise: one day at the hotel by myself and already the injuries were mounting. I figured I wouldn't be going to Otsuchi again.

But instead of telling me off, she simply said, "You need to be more careful out there."

It was my method that had gotten Kenichi up on the step stool, my recklessness that had led to his fractured collarbone. But, as Ise turned and went back inside the base camp, I realized she wasn't going to take me off the hotel. Maybe my look of surprise had convinced her the accident wasn't my fault, or maybe some divine luck had rubbed off on me from the Shinto prayers.

Accidents couldn't keep happening at the hotel, but, for now, I'd skated.

July 26

Two days later, in the morning, seven volunteers rode out with me to Otsuchi. Two were college kids who'd come with a group from Sophia University in Tokyo and arrived the morning after Kenichi's injury. For the students in the van, it would be their second day at the hotel, and I was determined to make sure they returned safely to the base camp that evening, though, my attempts to moderate our work had not been entirely successful.

The day before, I'd begun by asking the students to strip out everything in the entryway—a relatively safe, easy job—pointing out the trim around the windowsills and what remained of the aluminum supports on the ceiling after I'd taken out the tile. While they did this, I began gutting the rest of the main room; Kenichi and I had gotten quite a bit done, and I figured I could quickly finish off the rest using my ladder technique, which would be fine so long as I didn't involve the students. But, after seeing what had happened to Kenichi, I wore a hardhat and worked carefully, which slowed me down.

When I took a break and went to check on the students, I found they'd dragged a table into the entryway, and a boy was standing on top of it trying to use a pair of bolt cutters to snip one of the dead electrical wires running along the ceiling. Because the concrete floor beneath the table was uneven, it wobbled every time he moved, and he wore in a pair of rubber boots several sizes too small for him—his heels bulged out where his ankles should've been.

I wanted to yell at him, to tell him to never put himself in danger like that as long as he was within fifty feet of the hotel. But then, I hadn't exactly been a model of safety that morning. Instead, I asked if I could give it a shot, figuring at least this would get him off the table. He handed me the bolt cutters, and I climbed up in his place. I managed to get the pincers around the wire, but, when I started to squeeze, I felt my jaw flex involuntarily and my forearms went numb and shaky until it felt as though they were made of rubber.

The wire was live. Current still buzzing through my body, I lowered the bolt cutters and tried not to let my surprise show: I'd been a millimeter away from electrocuting myself.

"Let's leave it," I said, in my best nothing-to-see-here voice. If the students didn't know how much danger they'd been in, they'd have nothing to report. "We'll come back to this later."

We set about shoveling the rubble from the ceilings into wheelbarrows. The students weren't exactly experienced laborers, but they were young and strong. I was surprised at how carefully they listened to my instructions. I think I must have seemed like a savage, working in my filthy clothes, which I'd only washed twice since coming, stomping through the derelict hotel and throwing pieces of debris out the glassless windows onto the rubble piles outside. Though I was only a few years older than them, the ruined town was like an alien world compared with the orderly atmosphere of the city, and I must've seemed like an inhabitant of this foreign land; I couldn't help but feel a little proud of this.

The students and I were working together when a gray car pulled up in front of the hotel and Kenichi got out of the passenger side. I was surprised to see him—usually he would call the base camp and let me or one of the staff members know when he was coming. But I was relieved to see his arm wasn't bandaged. Maybe the break hadn't been so bad after all.

A man I'd never seen before got out of the driver's side, went over to him, and said something too softly for me to hear. Together, they came around the front of the car, and I said hello, but he didn't respond or even seem to recognize me. I offered to show him what we'd accomplished that morning, and he looked at me, finally seeming to notice I was there, though he still didn't seem to know who I was.

"What the hell are you all doing here?"

I tilted my head to one side. "What?"

"Who said you could be here?" he demanded.

I said he had. He wrinkled his nose at this and trumped upstairs. I couldn't understand what had just happened—why he was acting like this? Had he given himself a concussion as well? Confused, my sense of leadership shaken, I decided not to follow upstairs, and a great tiredness filled me. I turned back to work, hoping the students hadn't caught too much of what'd been said.

When Kenichi came back down on his way out, he again muttered, "What are you all doing here?"

The man with him took him by the arm and hurried out of the hotel. Stunned, I watched his car grow smaller on the road.

It wasn't until lunch, when I went to the Akazaki's place and told them about the visit, that Jun told me about Kenichi's younger brother; the two Michimata boys had a familial resemblance, and they'd often been mistaken for twins. As the eldest, Kenichi should've taken over the family businesses in Otsuchi, which included the hotel and a newspaper distributorship. But, after finding his Catholic faith, he'd gone his own way. His brother, who'd been an amateur sumo wrestler and later a police officer in the area around Tokyo, eventually returned home. He'd been running the Kotobuki Hotel along with his and Kenichi's mother-in-law when the quake struck, and the tsunami crashed down on the town. He'd survived, but their mother-in-law was still missing.

When I asked Kenichi, he'd say his brother had been a borderline alcoholic before, and the disaster had pushed him over the edge. His wife had divorced him, and, eventually, he wound up in a recovery clinic in Tokyo. He resented Kenichi's returning to Otsuchi to take over the family's interests, even if he wasn't in any shape to do so himself.

I was beginning to see that Kenichi was more complicated than his transparent, forward-looking manner suggested. He wasn't the type to talk much about his feelings, but this complete lack of interest in the photo album, which must've belonged to his younger brother, hinted at the depth of the rift between them.

When I went out to the lot where Kenichi always parked his Prius, I found the photo book still on the curb where he'd set it down the day before.

Despite these dents to my leadership, as I drove out the next morning, I was feeling optimistic. In addition to the two students, three Catholic brothers had arrived in the morning and decided to join us at the hotel. There were also two bikers in the van, who'd rolled into the parking lot below Kamaishi Catholic on their motorcycles the day before.

They were on a months-long road trip around northeastern Japan, and Kamaishi would be their third stint volunteering. Takayuki Kitahara was a big man with a square jaw, who looked like he could bolt down a bowl of ramen in one slurp. His riding partner, Ueshima, was wiry and shorter; he was quiet and often let Takayuki do the talking for both of them. Together, they cut a striking image in the dormitory. The bulk of the volunteers at the base camp were high school and college students or retirees and older people, and almost all of them were solidly middle-class. On the other hand, Takayuki and Ueshima's brush haircuts, rough accents, and beat-up leathers marked them as working-class guys. I figured at least one of them had construction experience and, indeed, over the following days, I'd learn that Takayuki was a security guard and Ueshima had worked for a building contractor. I needed their help if I was going to finish gutting the hotel by August, and, at the end of the evening meeting, I'd pointed out my project on the sign-up sheet to them.

After we arrived in Otsuchi, an electrician showed up, saying Kenichi had asked him to take a look at the building and see what needed to be rewired on the first floor. I asked him if he could tape up the cable near the entryway's ceiling and pointed out the spot where I'd scored the black insulation with the bolt cutters the day before.

The electrician got his ladder, and I showed everyone around the hotel, explaining what still needed to be done. The second floor still had to be pressure washed, and I also asked the college students to begin spraying down the first-floor entryway, even as I kept gutting the main room. We got to work, and, as the pressure-washing moved onto the second floor, water from upstairs found seams in the concrete and dripped down on the volunteers on the first floor who were ripping out the last walls and bits of trim. Though the electrician had wound some electrical tape around the live wire, I was still afraid we might all be electrocuted at any moment.

These conditions were an improvement but still far from ideal. I wasn't entirely surprised when, after lunch, Ueshima asked if we could have a brief meeting. I knew it wasn't going to be a painless process, but I said that sounded fine. We stood in a circle in the main room of the first floor, and Ueshima started by saying we needed to lay down a few rules.

"Working like we've been doing today is dangerous, plain and simple."

Already, my face was growing warm. Having the little authority I'd managed to scrape together from days and days of hard work challenged by a newcomer wasn't a good feeling. But I clenched my teeth and kept my hands folded behind my back. After all, if I couldn't admit when I was wrong, what kind of leader was I? Besides, I'd brought the bikers in, hoping they'd help shoulder the responsibility for the hotel project—who was I to complain when they did just that?

The meeting broke up after we'd established a few safety principals: inspect all electric cables and connections before using power tools, tape down extension cords when possible, immediately throw all debris into a wheelbarrow, and keep the floors clean. Afterward, Ueshima came over and asked what I'd thought of the meeting.

"I thought it was fine," I said, still smarting a bit. "It'll be better this way, right?"

He nodded, turned and went back to work. For as long as I knew him, Ueshima was a terse man, and he never gave you more words than he needed to make himself understood.

Following the rules slowed us down, and, at times, I was impatient to get on with our work. However, I also saw how these guidelines steadied our crew, removing the frantic energy from our labors. After we cleaned up, we stood in a circle and had another meeting in which everyone said what they'd gotten done that day. This was almost too by the book for me, but I swallowed hard and tried to get in the right frame of mind. I reminded myself how the whole point of coming to Tohoku had been to try to help in any way I could; I forced myself to see how unimportant my pride was.

On the drive back, I put the agitations of the day behind me. Everyone in the van was quiet, and I had no desire to talk either. I drove carefully and felt my sense of self dissipating into the landscape around me. By the time we got back to base camp, I'd made my peace with the bikers' roles in the project.

Not long after we arrived, Ise came to me in the parking lot while we were unloading the tools from the van and checking them off against the list we always took with us. She said I should be able to get some rest that night, because I didn't have to worry about working at the hotel tomorrow.

"You'll have a day off," she said.

"A day off? Who's going to drive out there?" Of course, what I meant was, who could possibly take over for me?

"I'm sure Ueshima or Kitahara can handle it."

Her tone and the way she nodded said there'd be no debating the matter.

So that was it. All the work I'd done on the hotel, and still my jurisdiction over it had been stripped away with such ease. A wave of fury rose through me, but even as it rolled over me, a swell of exhaustion crashed down on top of it.

I left the details of unloading the van to the other volunteers, staggered inside, and went to the dorm room where I slept at night. I wanted to take off running: to run through the ruins left by the tsunami, to run into the hills above the city, to run until I was high above and far away from the nearest human voice.

Instead, I tore off my clothes and collapsed onto my futon.

July 27

In the morning light, I saw Ise was right. I'd been wrapped up in the idea of being the driver for the project, but, ultimately, what mattered was the work, not my own conceit.

More important was the fact that I'd been working at the hotel for eight days straight and every night I came back to the base camp exhausted. After a bath and dinner, I could barely keep my eyes open through the evening meeting. Though I slept eight or nine hours a night, I was still tired. I was too tired to wash my clothes or make a lunch any more complicated than a can of tuna and several balls of rice. I was too tired to call Junko, and it had been days since we'd spoken.

The longer-term volunteers were all required to take rest days. The day before had been Hiramatsu's day off. It had been a warm night and, between Takayuki, Ueshima, the college students, and the rest of the volunteers, the women's dorm had been crowded and stuffy during the evening meeting. Hiramatsu sat in the middle of the room in his linen pajamas, using a worn paper fan to swat away the flying ants that had gotten inside. Without the hotel to think about, all the tension left my body, and I soaked up the atmosphere, which was like a packed theater in the minutes before a performance, people saying hello on their way to their seats or chatting with the person next to them.

In the morning, I didn't know what to do with myself. I'd woken after all the other volunteers had left for the day, and I wandered through the deserted rectory and wound up looking at a Kamaishi sightseeing pamphlet that had been left on a desk in the hall. Driving on the highway, on one or two occasions I'd seen what looked like a brilliant white tower on a hill across the bay from the base camp. Now, I saw it was actually a giant statue of the Kannon, the Buddhist god of mercy. I decided to pay it a visit and took a city bus that wound through the hills on Kamaishi's southern coast.

I spent the morning looking at the relics in a small museum at the base of the statue, which included a tiny, mummified bone supposedly taken from the corpse of the historical Buddha himself. Afterward, I sat on a bench outside and thought about my grandfather and tried to write down my impressions of the tsunami-affected area in the journal I'd brought with me.

In the afternoon, I returned to the base camp and decided to get a haircut. The last time I'd talked to Junko, I'd mentioned how long my hair was getting, how it kept falling into my eyes when I worked. She sent me a link to a magazine article about a man who'd reopened his salon in the disaster area, though his building didn't have electricity or running water. This stylist was Keitaro Matsumoto, and while he cut my hair, I asked if he'd been at his salon on the day of the disaster. He was skillful at describing his experience of the tsunami, and I figured talking to his customers probably gave him plenty of chances to practice telling his story. My instinct was to jot down what he was saying, though I wasn't sure how he'd feel about me using his story, and, once I started working at the hotel again, I'd be too exhausted to do any writing.

After the haircut, Keitaro and I exchanged contact information. I still had a couple hours before the evening meeting and decided to wash off the trimmings of hair that had stuck to me in Tsuru-no-Yu. The bathhouse had also been damaged in the tsunami but reopened not long before I arrived. The base camp hosted well over a dozen volunteers on any given day, and we couldn't all shower at the rectory. Instead, we were given tickets to the bathhouse, which was only a couple minutes' walk away.

The outside of the bathhouse had separate entrances for men and women. The changing area had been built as a single room but was divided by a partition that ran the length of the space, save for a few feet where a booth had been built in between the entry doors and against the front wall. This allowed the manager to collect the bathing fees and make change for both genders, and a few well-placed curtains prevented anyone from catching a glimpse of the other side. Day after day, the same middle-aged woman sat in this booth collecting money. Next to the lockbox, she had a small color TV that was constantly tuned to variety shows, which she only half watched while she looked out on her naked customers, a tired expression on her face as if she was exhausted by this parade of human flesh.

A sliding glass door led from the men's changing room to the bathing area, where waist-high showerheads were mounted on low tiled walls. There were short plastic stools stacked by the door, and, having undressed, I took one and sat and washed myself before rinsing off and taking a dip in one of the two rectangular tile baths in back. The water in one of the tubs was almost painfully hot, just the way I liked it, while the other tub could be made cooler by twisting a cold-water spigot that jutted out from the wall. While I soaked, I liked to watch the customers who came for their evening dip.

During my time in Kamaishi, the most outlandish group I saw there was a dozen or so bearded men who'd entered the changing room just after I finished stripping down one day. As usual, I'd been working at the hotel, and this normally meant I was the filthiest person in the bathhouse. But these guys' stench—a sour, condensed, bodily funk—was practically a physical presence in the room. And yet, their matching clothing and the worn wooden walking stick one of them carried suggested they weren't simply destitute. I tried not to stare and went into the bathing area, where I showered and then lowered myself into the hotter of the two tubs. The warmth was spreading through my body when one of the men climbed into the tub next to me. I turned to the starved-looking man and asked where he and his group were from. It turned out they were monks. They'd walked all the way from Tokyo on a pilgrimage to honor the victims of the disaster. They'd been walking for a month and, each night, they stayed in a Buddhist temple in whichever town they reached.

But even more fascinating to me than these outsiders, were the bathhouse regulars whose relationships and personalities I tried to puzzle out evening by evening. There was one man with a tattoo stretching over his shoulder blades of a crazed samurai running a sword through a demon snake. People with tattoos weren't usually allowed in public baths, as they were a mark of organized crime affiliations, but these rules sometimes went unenforced in close-knit communities. I enjoyed looking at the illustration, how it moved as he furiously scrubbed his sides. Another of the regulars was a man who seemed to be in his fifties and wore his gray hair in a military crew cut. Most nights he was accompanied by a bald man with only a few white wisps on his age-spotted pate, and the middle-aged man would order his elderly companion around, telling him to sit, rinse off, get in the water, get out, and so on. Their routine was to shower, get in the hot water for a few minutes, and then the younger man would wash his elder's back—a sign of filial respect. When they performed this last part of their ritual, the older man, who I assumed was the younger man's father, would stand with his eyes closed and his arms hanging limply by his sides while his son scrubbed him from his shoulders to his hips as if he were a giant nude infant. I wondered if the older man was still all there, how well he was able to distinguish one day from the next.

However, on my day off, I went the bathhouse earlier than usual and didn't see any of these familiar faces. Instead, by myself in the hot water, I had time to consider that these were my last days in Kamaishi. Junko had said there might be another chance to do a couple part-time jobs for a friend of hers, but I needed to be back in Mutsu by the beginning of August. I'd told Ise I would be leaving on the second, which was only five days away.

As I toweled off in the changing room, I dreaded the idea of leaving. The disaster had destroyed so much, left so much uncertainty behind, but it had also broken down the barriers between people. At the base camp, how much money you made didn't matter, how high up you were in your company or where you were from didn't matter.

I was thinking of Hiramatsu and Ise, who'd watched over me so carefully during my time there, of Takayuki and Ueshima, who'd be back at the base camp, of Father Toru and Tanizawa, who'd be sitting with their legs tucked under them in the women's dorm room as they waited for the evening meeting to start. Though I'd gotten caught up volunteering at the hotel, it was the sense of community between the volunteers I enjoyed. When I first arrived in Kamaishi, in the back of my mind I'd hoped the experience might help me understand my faith, but in all my time in the disaster area, the closest I came was seeing how—though it was often buried under the trials of everyday life—my belief was bound up in those whom I connected with. I found people endlessly interesting and beautiful, and coming together with them was the best way I had of being part of something greater than myself.

There was a shortcut back to the church, a dirt alley snaking between a few houses. I darted between the stepping-stones on the dark path, knowing that in less than a week I'd heft my backpack onto my shoulders, Ise would drive me to the station, and I'd get on a train that would take me far away from Kamaishi. Once again, I'd be on my own, just a few thousand yen to my name.

July 31

For days, shipments of supplies had been arriving at the hotel. Unable to help out himself, Kenichi had taken to ordering boxes of work gloves, stacks of futon pads, and vacuum cleaners.

I wasn't entirely surprised when, two days later, a truck driver wandered into the hotel looking for someone to sign for a delivery. I scrawled my name on the invoice, which was for two portable toilets. The bikers and I helped the driver unload them from his truck, but then we had to move them to the locations marked on a map of the area that the driver had been given. The porta-potties hadn't been used, but, with tanks full of disinfectant fluid, they were enormously heavy. We couldn't tilt them for fear of spilling the fluid, so, to move one, the four of us hunched over to lift them from the bottom and grunted and panted as we shuffled a hundred meters down the road.

Back at the hotel, work was wrapping up. We'd ripped every board and composite panel out of the first floor, and all we needed to do was finish spraying the space down with the pressure washer. We stayed on the premises for lunch, and I sat cross-legged on a tarp that Takayuki had unfolded in the front room on the second floor. From the cooler, he took out a rice ball bigger than his own head and stretched his mouth as wide as he could to bite into the corner. I'd also gotten used to eating enormous portions while working at the hotel, as the work always left me ravenous, and I'd wind up eating two or three times more than usual.

After lunch, Kenichi's Prius pulled into the parking lot across from the hotel. He got out of the passenger side, a cloth sling around his right arm. He moved slowly, unsteadily, and didn't immediately start trudging forward in his usual head-down way. I hesitated to go to him.

A few days before, while doing the last of the demolitions on the first floor, I'd noticed a small wooden shelf high up in one of the back corners. I pulled down on it with a crowbar, until the wood splintered, and clumps of dried mud came spilling down—I heard glass shatter at my feet. Gold specks glittered on the floor and an alcohol smell rose up. Sifting through the dirt, I came up with a folded calligraphy paper and a Ziploc bag of coins and a thick bankroll of cash.

In my old homestay family's house, there had also been a small enclave in a corner of one of the inner rooms next to the family's Buddhist shrine. A *kami-dana*, where offerings to the Shinto spirits were kept: fruit, sweets, and little bottles of ceremonial sake with gold leaf mixed in. I hadn't realized a business would have one as well.

I was around the corner from where Takayuki and Ueshima were working, and I counted the money once and then a second time. There was the equivalent of a little over two hundred dollars: to me it was a fortune. With that kind of money, I could stay in Kamaishi and keep volunteering instead of returning to Mutsu to work some shady, under-the-table job for minimum wage. Instead of taking the overnight bus, I could ride the Shinkansen back to Tokyo in order to catch my plane back to the States. Surely, the money had belonged to Kenichi's alcoholic brother or, more likely, his mother-in-law, who was still missing. Technically, the cash should go to Kenichi, since he was the next of kin, but I'd worked hard at the hotel, and this would repay only a few days of my labor. Why shouldn't I take it? Why not just quietly fold the bills into my pocket?

I hadn't come to the tsunami-affected area to steal from the survivors, but no one would notice if I peeled off a couple of the big bills. Or even just one.

Three days later, I had the Ziploc bag in my hand while I watched Kenichi and his son getting out of the car across the street. For the past two nights, before leaving for the day, I'd taken the money out from under the pile of salvaged photos and water-stained account books where I kept it and left it on one of the glassless windowsills where anyone could see it. I hoped I'd return the next day to find it missing—to find someone had taken it, or it had simply disappeared. But both times, after driving out to Otsuchi, I made sure I was the first out of the van and hustled over to back window where I'd left the bag. Both times it was there.

Oh, if I could just take the fucking money.

But I couldn't. If I did, somehow, I knew it would spoil every memory I had of Otsuchi and the base camp; whenever I thought of those weeks, all I would think of would be the Ziploc bag. I cursed myself for ever finding the cash.

I bit my bottom lip and crossed the street. I went to Kenichi and asked how he was.

"Fine, fine," he said. "Today I've got my boy driving. This is Kei."

I introduced myself, though Kei avoided my eyes and mumbled his greeting. Kenichi had told me about his three boys, and, over the years, as I got to know his family better, I'd learn Kei was the middle child. Unlike the eldest son, who worked for a big company in Sendai, Kei hadn't stuck with any one line of work for long and still lived near his parents.

I stepped in close to Kenichi, said I'd found something, and handed over the bag to him. I wasn't sure what I'd expected. Maybe that his eyes would go wide, and he'd thank me excitedly, or that he'd hand me the money back and insist I keep it precisely because I'd thought to return it. He did neither though, and, instead, nodded to himself, then turned and opened the car door a crack and threw the bag on the passenger seat.

"The wood is coming today," he said, having already forgotten it.

I did my best to smile and nod, though I couldn't help wincing.

My work, I tried to remind myself, was almost done. In two weeks, the hotel had gone from being a wreck to looking as if it had just been built. The bare, washed concrete was a satisfying sight, and I enjoyed walking the footprint of the building, uncluttered by any debris or walls. The day before, I'd nailed a piece of junk plywood to a long-plank, and, in my blocky script, I wrote out a sign asking anyone who went upstairs to take off their shoes on the third floor.

Before long, a truck arrived with a bed full of long boards. Kenichi had arranged for a carpenter to come up from Tokyo, and he was going to use the wood to refurbish the hotel, building shelves, fitting new doors, and framing the windows. Kenichi told his son to go up to the second floor, and Takayuki and I handed the planks up to him, in which he pulled them in through one of the windows. Kenichi shouted directions from below, telling Kei where to put the boards and how to stack them. Kei shook his head, and I figured he was conditioned to his father's hard-charging style.

In spite of his injury, Kenichi was as full of energy as ever, happy to lose himself in some bit of work. He wasn't yet thinking of the sacrifices he'd have to make: moving his family back to his hometown, uprooting his wife, waking up before dawn to manage his family's newspaper distributorship, and, eventually, watching the hotel we'd worked so hard to save be torn down. He didn't know that, when he pulled Kei into the project of reviving the family businesses, the pressure would weigh on his son. He didn't know how dark it would get; he didn't know how Kei would take his own life, hanging himself in their newly built home.

Kenichi didn't yet know how much hardship still lay ahead. None of us did.

What I knew was that the sun had come out. In a few days, I would see Junko, and, though our relationship was on uncertain ground, we were still together. And, in that moment, I was happy to be with Kenichi, Takayuki, and Ueshima, watching something new come together in the middle of the ruins—in spite of all the horrible things that had happened and all the difficulties we were yet to face, I was glad to see how calamity, death, and loss could give way to possibility, even hope.

Reconstruction

September 2011-February 2017

I. The Village of Two Stones

Kamaishi City, Iwate Prefecture

The summer after the disaster, Junko's father was dying. He'd been sick since before the tsunami, but, afterward, his health turned for the worse. When the doctors first diagnosed him, they'd said he might live a few years or as little as six months. He was sixty-six and, until the cancer, had been in good health. He was too young for this.

After I finished working as a volunteer in Kamaishi and Otsuchi, I stayed in northeastern Japan for a few weeks, working under the table, attending local summer festivals, and sneaking off to visit Junko, lending her what comfort I could. Once I returned to the States in September, Junko and I resumed our nightly phone calls, though she didn't talk much about her father's condition. When she did mention her dad's most recent checkup or the experimental treatment they were considering for him, I tried not to pry. Having lost my grandfather when I was separated from my family and still getting to know the other volunteers at the base camp, I understood there are times when grief is a private affair. But I also wondered if she and I weren't drifting apart and if it wasn't better to let the distance creep in.

I worried our relationship was like a ghost haunting us, keeping us from paying attention to our lives—her last months with her father, my graduate program in Ohio. I wanted so badly to be successful in my writing, and I'd heard from the faculty and the older students that the writers who blossomed into the stars of the program were those who threw themselves into their work, often suffering some kind of traumatic breakdown followed by a transformation: a terrible and cathartic experience. Talking to Junko every night, still being emotionally attached to her, meant I was in some way immune to the currents carrying along my peers, who would often go missing for days at a time only to reappear at one of the grad student parties, hook up with one another, and then go their separate ways, all the while presumably growing as artists.

Though I sometimes regretted the entanglements I'd arrived in Columbus with, I owed Junko something. I needed to see her again to figure out where we stood.

We were still keeping in touch when her father passed in early October. She called me from her car in the parking lot outside the hospital. I could hear in her voice how badly his death had broken her. I tried to think of anything to say, words I might wrap around her like an embrace, but the best I could do was to listen. Even as his being gone hurt her to the core, she seemed relieved to see him finally released from the way the pain had warped him. I asked if she was okay driving home on her own and she assured me she'd be fine. He was watching over her now.

Over the next couple weeks, she told me about the preparations her family was making for her father's burial. His body was cleaned, and he was dressed in a black kimono crossed right over left, opposite the way the living dress. He was brought home for a traditional Buddhist wake, so friends and family could pay their respects; incense was burned over him, and the local priest was summoned to say prayers. For the funeral, his body was cremated, and Junko, her sisters, and mother used oversized wooden chopsticks to pick his bones out from the piles of ash and place them in an urn. Finally, his remains were interred in a stone monument that was erected in the hillside cemetery in Junko's hometown, where her mother would one day be buried and where she and her sisters could visit him anytime they liked. With each symbolic act, Junko was saying goodbye to her father as she had known him—his living, breathing form— and coming to think of him as a spirit who watched over the family he'd left behind. Each ritual helped her accept this transition and feel he was still present in her life.

I'd listened to Junko describe each step of her father's burial, so when I returned to Japan in the winter after the tsunami and met Keitaro Matsumoto, I understood why he was uneasy that his mother's body still hadn't been found. In most sects of Japanese Buddhism, the body is central, and the burial ceremonies serve as containers for the grief of the bereaved.

I'd kept in touch with Keitaro as well as with Kenichi Michimata, who would let me know about the progress being made at the hotel. After I'd left, a Korean carpenter, who was also Catholic, had volunteered his time to come and renovate the first two floors. With Kenichi's blessing, a priest from Nagasaki had then moved into the hotel to establish the Caritas Japan Otsuchi Base Camp. I was eager to see what the hotel would look like, to catch up with Keitaro, Jun, and Michimata, and to see how the recovery effort was moving forward. I had about a month off from my graduate program and had been checking the prices of flights to Tokyo. I found a good deal and figured I could squeeze in a visit to Japan before Christmas. Once I'd seen how things were in Iwate, I planned to keep heading north to Aomori to meet Junko and pay my respects at her father's grave.

This time, after taking the Shinkansen north from Tokyo, I transferred to a local train and was late getting into Kamaishi. By the time I arrived and checked the transit schedule in the station's waiting room, I saw the last bus for Otsuchi had already gone. As usual, I was traveling on a tight budget. I took all the cash out of my wallet, counted it, and pushed my hand with the money into my pocket before walking out to the parking lot, where I approached a taxi idling a few feet from the station.

When I asked the driver how much it would be to get to the hotel, he said, "All the way out there?"

He looked at the screen of his navigation system, tapped at it for a moment, and then quoted me a price well above the sweaty sum in my fist. I thanked him and went back inside the station. I had the number of the priest who was staying at the hotel but calling him out of the blue and asking him to come pick me up would be rude. I didn't want to start out on the wrong foot. I also had Keitaro's number, and he knew I was in the area.

Back in the summer, after I finished my first stint as a volunteer, but before I'd left Japan on my way south, I'd visited his temporary housing unit. He'd been assigned a place to live in August, and I'd come, hoping he'd let me record him as I asked a few questions.

I wasn't sure what I would do with the recording; I mostly wrote fiction—short stories, a couple unfinished novels, a failed poem here and there. But his story amazed me, not just because of what had happened to him during the tsunami, but because of what had come after, the way he'd picked himself up and tried to move on. By his own account, he was an ordinary man, and his experience was a window into the reality of thousands of people in Tohoku. Having worked with survivors the summer after the tsunami, to me the real drama of the disaster seemed to be about what came after the waters receded: the hundreds of thousands of individual struggles to find a way forward, which, collectively, made up the reconstruction effort.

Part of this undertaking was the clusters of temporary housing that had been thrown up with lightning speed all over the city, the entire region. These shelters for the dispossessed were typically single-story structures with sheet metal roofs, arranged back-to-back in rows that could stretch on for the length of a soccer field. Each unit was about the width of a single-wide trailer, but only a quarter as long. In some clusters, there were larger multi-room units for families, units with yards for survivors with pets, and units with wheelchair ramps and easy nursing home access for the elderly. Some clusters were home to a few dozen survivors, while others had been built to house hundreds, thousands even. Altogether, in the year after the disaster, over half a million people found themselves living in temporary housing.

Keitaro's unit was in a complex in the south of the city, near the coast, that had been built on a sports park next to an open-air baseball stadium. One of the reasons he'd been recommended to this cluster was because it had a central pavilion with commercial spaces, where survivors who'd lost stores could reestablish their businesses.

In the summer, when I visited him in his prefab unit, not long after he moved in, I'd planned to get back on the local train and return to the Shinkansen line in the evening. But it was almost dark by the time I got off the city bus at the stop in front of his housing cluster. The trip had taken longer than I'd planned, and I worried about where I'd stay if I didn't make the last train. As soon as I met him though, he assured me I could sleep at his place if needed.

He led me across the gravel parking lot and showed me inside his unit. The front door opened into a tiny kitchen, which was also the hallway to the main room. The total floor space was smaller than a truck bed, though he'd somehow managed to fit all his belongings inside. He cooked us dinner using a meal kit, so all he had to do was chop a few vegetables, stir-fry them with some minced meat, and then add a prepackaged sauce to this mixture. He had an entire box of these dinners and, like his television and his futon pads, they had been donated from around the country. In spite of these amenities, there was no getting around the size of the unit or the uninsulated walls, which were so thin I could make out the commercials playing on his neighbor's TV. After our interview, Keitaro and I lay down side by side and went to sleep in his tiny living room. In the middle of the night, I woke to a chill in the air and had to search out an extra blanket to wrap myself in.

In December, three months later, I dialed Keitaro's number on the payphone inside Kamaishi Station; I could imagine the white-breath cold of the room where his cell phone was ringing. When he picked up, I told him I was at the train station and asked if he could give me a lift to Otsuchi. He was surprised but quickly agreed, and, despite the cold, I went outside to wait for him.

In the months since I'd seen Keitaro, I'd used our interview to write an account of his experience of the disaster. I wasn't sure if I was going to try to publish this piece, but in the process of describing what he'd been through, I'd come to empathize with him and wanted to know how he was doing, how far along the reconstruction effort had brought him.

After a few minutes, Keitaro pulled into the roundabout in front of the station in the boxy gold Honda that he'd bought secondhand to replace the car he'd lost in the tsunami. He came around from the driver's side, and I smiled and bowed and shook his hand. He opened the rear door, and I slung my frame pack from my shoulders and onto the backseat, then climbed into the passenger side. He settled in behind the wheel, both of our faces lit by the instrument panel as he drove us through the dark city.

Volunteering at Kamaishi Catholic, I'd been under a curfew and had rarely seen the city at night, but it was beautiful to look across the dark water and see the sparkling streetlights on the far side of the bay, their reflections trembling in the cold, dark water below the shore. While Keitaro piloted us down the main street, I began to make out familiar sights—the yellow-lit windows of the Sun Route Hotel, the Lawson's convenience store where I'd often come to call Junko—and new structures: a chain *izakaya*, a local Chinese restaurant, and several just-finished homes, all of which had garages only on the first floor.

We passed an empty lot, where the building that had housed Keitaro's salon had stood until it was demolished a couple weeks before. The structure had been condemned for several months and he'd known it was going to be torn down. Still, it hurt to see it go.

After a few blocks, Keitaro turned left and drove up a hill and onto the highway on-ramp. The road flowed into the Tenjin Tunnel and we began catching up as he drove. He was making plans to reopen Hair Studio K in one of his temporary housing cluster's commercial spaces, but it wouldn't be easy. While the space was free, it was just an empty room. All the furniture from his former salon—the mirror, the chair, cabinet for storing his scissors, combs, and blow dryer—had been lost to the tsunami, as had almost all his beauty supplies. He had to buy hairpins, dyes, spray, wax, shampoo and conditioner, but how was he supposed to afford them when he was barely scraping by as it was? Moreover, Keitaro's salon had been part of a community, he'd been dependent on regular customers, and now his clients were scattered all over the city, the prefecture, if they were alive at all.

On top of this, he was anxious about his mother, Nobuko, who was still missing. When several weeks had gone by without her being found in any of the evacuation shelters or refugee camps, and without her body surfacing, the authorities had declared her dead. In the area where Ryoishi had once been, the only evidence of her they'd found was a scarf. There were no remains to burn and put in the family plot, but he'd attended a memorial ceremony for the victims of the disaster and said the Buddhist prayers for her.

"It was all I could do," Keitaro had told me when I'd visited him in his cramped temporary housing unit.

Now, as he drove, he told me that human remains were still washing up from the ocean. The police would do DNA testing on whatever fragments they could find, and Keitaro and his brother had both submitted cheek swabs with the hope of finding a match.

I was amazed at how matter-of-factly Keitaro said all this, how openly he could talk about what I imagined were incredibly painful things for him. I wasn't sure what to say, or if I should ask him more or let the subject drop. I decided on the latter as we approached the end of the tunnel.

I still remembered the roads in the area from the many times I'd driven them as a volunteer. During those weeks, I'd learned every curve of the two routes that lead from Kamaishi out to the hotel in Otsuchi: the new National Highway 45 ran inland and went through several tunnels beneath the steep foothills while an older version of the same road hugged the coast, going through Ryoishi. The hamlet where Keitaro's childhood home had been was once its own village, though it merged into Kamaishi in the late 1800s. The name Ryoishi literally meant "both rocks," or, as I'd come to think of it, "the village of two stones."

Driving out of the tunnel, Keitaro slowed as we approached the stoplight where the two routes diverged. When I'd been there over the summer, I'd been stunned by Ryoishi. The degree of erasure was unlike anything I'd seen. Most of the houses had been so completely pulverized that only their exposed foundations marked where homes had once stood; rebar-reinforced telephone poles meant to withstand hurricanes lay bent in half; even the road's asphalt had been torn out of the ground and broken chunks lay here and there like scattered puzzle pieces. For me, the enormous concrete seawall, which the waves had partially toppled over, was symbolic of a catastrophic failure of imagination, an inability to comprehend the power of forces of nature. Within minutes of the first tremors, any human illusion of control had melted into air.

And so, before the light turned green, I asked Keitaro if we could take the old highway through Ryoishi. "What's it like now?" I wondered.

Only after Keitaro had started driving straight ahead, toward his hometown, did I consider that it might be difficult for him to revisit the place where his mother had been before the waves swept her away. But we were already past the turnoff, and I thought bringing it up might only make matters worse.

We drove over a bridge, high above a river that ran perpendicular to the road. Looking to the right, beyond Keitaro's silhouette, I could see the dark mountain of rubble, large as two soccer fields and several stories high, and I remembered how I'd watched excavators and dump trucks crawling over it like ants all summer. This massive pile had shrunk since I'd seen it, and I figured they were starting to ship the debris out on river barges.

We crested a small hill and came to a stoplight set up on a tripod; a few hundred yards down the road, there was another light like this. Both were set on timers, which allowed traffic to travel in one direction for a couple minutes before one light switched to red and then, after a delay, the other switched to green, reversing the flow. This limited traffic to a single lane, allowing construction crews to repave the other side.

When the light turned, we started down the long slope, and, on the right, the form of the seawall appeared, growing taller as the hill took us further down. The wall had been built after an experiment in the mid-seventies showed the breakers planned for Kamaishi's main port would deflect waves to Ryoishi. In 2009, the breakers in Kamaishi, which had been under construction for over half of Keitaro's life, had finally been finished. Two years later, these coastal defenses were overwhelmed by the tsunami in a matter of minutes. Likewise, a sixty-foot wave decimated the barrier at Ryoishi. While the local officials said Kamaishi's breakers didn't increase the size of the waves that struck the surrounding communities, Keitaro didn't believe these denials.

At the bottom of the hill, the road curved left. I could see the hole in the seawall. When we entered the village, much of the jumbled debris was gone, and the bare floor of the valley spread out around us.

"Our house was over there," Keitaro pointed off into the darkness beyond the windshield.

I looked to where he'd pointed, glad for the steadiness in his voice, but the only thing I saw was the thick black night. "Where?"

"Here," he stopped the car, shifted into park, and opened his door, the engine still running.

I climbed out and the cold cut through my down jacket and filled my lungs. Keitaro came around the front of the car, pointing to a bare concrete foundation elevated a few feet above those around it. I was stunned by the cold and by how changed the landscape was with the wreckage cleared away. In the hills, the houses that had escaped destruction were dark, their windows cracked or broken, a few of their doors hung ajar. The village was gone. I wondered what Keitaro felt, looking at the ruins of his home. And yet, he didn't seem too disturbed.

The best way I could articulate these thoughts was to nod and mutter, "I see."

Keitaro went back around to the driver's side. As I turned to get back in the car, I caught a glimpse of the seawall and, through the long gap where the barrier had been breached, the dark, moonlit ocean behind it. The broken chunks of concrete were gone. Only the undamaged segments of the barrier remained, and, even in the dark, I could see where the earth between the two intact sections of wall had been flattened and prepared for new construction.

They were actually rebuilding it. The seawall had failed so spectacularly—some of the people who'd escaped into the hills above Ryoishi had taken videos of the bay filling like a bowl, until the water spilled over the rim, crashing down into the streets, flooding the houses until their roofs disappeared under the water. In one of the videos that had been posted online, you could hear a man yelling, "This is hell! This is hell!" Not only had the seawall failed, but it may have even contributed to the loss of life by giving people a false sense of security and blocking their view of the ocean, preventing them from seeing the warning signs of a tsunami, like the extreme low tide in the minutes before the wave arrived. If Keitaro's mother had been able to look outside and see how far the sea level had retreated, maybe she would have known to flee. Maybe she would still be alive.

But the local government had decided to repair the wall, giving the rationale that it was the most cost-effective option. The city had also started rebuilding the damaged breakwaters in Kamaishi Bay, despite the critics who pointed out that this was throwing away money on technology that was a proven failure.

As Keitaro drove us through the center of the village, we passed where the last cluster of homes had been, and then the highway curved to the left again, before cutting sharply to the right, switchbacking up the steep rise that separated Ryoishi from the next neighborhood over. In the middle of this curve was a space about the size of a tennis court, where six inscribed stones had been mounted on a cement base. The first time I'd seen this monument, I guessed these rocks were the village's namesake.

When I asked, Keitaro said they were memorials to the previous tsunamis. Before they'd been moved from their original locations and collected in the back of the village, each stone had marked how high the waves had reached. Before modernity uprooted them, and before the seawall had been built, the stones had served as a warning to generations of villagers, telling them how far up the hill to evacuate after an earthquake. In a way, this system had worked: in 1896, a tsunami had killed three quarters of Ryoishi's population, but, when another earthquake struck the region in 1933, two years before Keitaro's mother was born, the villagers were prepared. The people managed an orderly evacuation and only three lost their lives.

Similar tsunami stones can be found up and down Japan's northeastern coast, and, in societies around the world, stones have long been used for memorials. No matter how tragic an event, people soon begin to forget, but stones hold our memories; when we come back and stand before them, they tell of the world as it once was and will never be again.

This was what I felt a week later, when I stood in the cold graveyard in Junko's hometown, in front of the granite resting place of her father. I hadn't known him, but a deep sense of quiet came over Junko as she moved her eyes over the characters of his name. She clasped her hands together and bowed her head; I think, in her mind, he came alive again for her in that moment.

The feelings brought on by such memories are raw, not easy to carry around, not suited to everyday life. Nine months after the disaster, much like his hometown, Keitaro was still struggling to find a clear path forward, making an attempt to restart his business and rebuild his life. A person couldn't constantly carry the weight of grief with them while doing that. I figured Keitaro had hidden his own emotions away, until his mother was found, and he could give her a proper burial.

Though it would take a couple more months, eventually the police would get in touch with him and his brother, letting them know they'd found a set of remains with DNA matching their samples. So many people had perished in the tsunami that there was no room in the morgues, and her body had been cremated. The cops had taken a photo though, which they presented to Keitaro to confirm his mother's identity. She didn't look the way he remembered her—she'd been one of the most beautiful women in the hamlet when he was young—but it was his mother.

In January, the year after the disaster, Nobuko Matsumoto's bones were interred in the family gravestone, in the small hillside cemetery behind Ryoishi. In the carved stone, Keitaro could leave some part of his loss, knowing he could always come back and find it.

Years later, when I returned to the area and took a closer look at Ryoishi's tsunami stones, I saw the village's forebears had done the same. One stone reads:

This memorial will eventually be destroyed, but our anguish will never be extinguished. This stone will speak for years to come, it will pass our sorrow down to our children and grandchildren. In year 29 of the Meiji Emperor, 709 persons were killed in Ryoishi Village by a massive wave. Only 204 were left alive after this calamity. God, how horrible.

II. The Wild-Horse Chase Festival

Minami-Soma, Iwate Prefecture

For three and a half years following the disaster, Katsue and Tsuneo Sakai had lived with their cat, Coo, in a temporary housing complex next to a park called Kame Koen. After fleeing from the area around the nuclear plant and living as refugees in a high school gymnasium in Koriyama for several weeks, they'd stayed at the Nekoma Hotel for four months. When the complex they were slated to live in was completed, they moved to Aizu-Wakamatsu City, two hours by car from their home in Okuma.

They were glad to have a place to stay and for the compensation money they received monthly from TEPCO. At the same time, the cleanup and reconstruction plans adopted by the electric utility and the government kept them trapped in a kind of purgatory.

Unwilling to write-off the towns around the plant, and thereby acknowledge the severity of the disaster, the government had embarked on a campaign to clean the land around Fukushima Daiichi. Day after day, men in protective clothing worked with heavy machinery, taking the topsoil off the fields, sweeping up the dirt and leaves, and gathering the radiation-contaminated material in enormous black plastic bags, which were stacked in sprawling piles around the countryside. While these workers were thorough enough, there was simply no way to clean entire forests, entire mountains. They could do their best, but, inevitably, the rain would fall, the wind would blow, and plumes of contaminated dust would resettle in fresh layers around the towns. In addition, the laborers brought in to do this cleaning—which included homeless people recruited by subcontractors from nearby cities such as Sendai—could work for only so long before they'd absorbed their yearly limit of radiation, and then they'd be let go. All this work gave the impression of progress, but it wasn't clear how much was really being accomplished.

As a result, the plans about when the evacuation orders would be lifted were uncertain at best. Most acknowledged it would be decades before the central districts in several of the towns would be habitable again. In the meantime, plans were developed to build new housing on the least contaminated areas of each town, to give those who wanted to move back a place to live. But this construction also faced delays.

With the government insistently promising they would someday be allowed back, and the Sakais' own desire to return home, they hadn't put down roots in Aizu-Wakamatsu. About five months after the triple meltdown at Fukushima Daiichi, a managing director from Tokyo Energy Systems, the TEPCO subcontractor Tsuneo had worked for at the nuclear plant, called and asked him to come back to work. But without a place to live near the plant, he couldn't commit to leaving his mother for an unknown amount of time, and so his position had been eliminated. He was out of work. Tsuneo and Katsue had both taken on various jobs, but these were usually part-time or temporary. They didn't know many locals, and, though Aizu-Wakamatsu was in the same prefecture as their hometown, the food and dialect were nothing like the area where they were from on the coast. Stark, snow-capped peaks surrounded the city like the walls of a fortress. After three years in the mountains, Katsue was tired of looking at them.

While she and her son waited to see what was next, time wasn't standing still. Coo was getting old, and Tsuneo was now firmly in his middle years; at thirty-five, he was around the age when many men get married, but how could he find someone knowing he'd someday ask them to move to Okuma with him? And when he did move, what kind of a future would be waiting for him? He didn't have a permanent job or even a home to speak of.

Despite this, Katsue remained determined to return home. Many of the other evacuees had resigned themselves to the fact that they would never go back to Okuma and moved to other prefectures to restart their lives or started looking for permanent positions in companies in the places they'd been relocated to. Some people had built new houses, others had gone off to live with relatives, but not Katsue.

In his own way, Tsuneo had also maintained his connections to their hometown, riding each year in Soma's Noma-Oi Matsuri or the Wild-Horse Chase Festival. Over the last weekend in July, the coastal area around Minami-Souma City played host to cavalry parades, horse races, and even a mounted capture the flag competition. Teams of horsemen and women came from all the surrounding towns, including Okuma. In 2011, with the entire region still reeling, the events had been canceled, but, in the year following the disaster, the festival resumed. Three years later, Junko and I went to see Tsuneo ride in the procession.

We drove down in the old diesel Toyota Corona I'd bought after moving to Sendai. After my master's program, I'd been given a year-long grant to do research on the reconstruction effort. Junko and I were in a good place, following a rough patch. Traffic was light, and we smiled at each other now and again as we zipped down the highway. But my year in Japan was almost up, and, in two weeks, I'd once again be getting on a plane and flying an ocean away from her.

I had first met Tsuneo in Aizu-Wakamatsu, when Junko and I volunteered for a weekend with a group called Ashiyu-tai that went to temporary housing units, giving footbaths and offering a place where the displaced could come, have a cup of coffee, and chat. I'd found volunteering in different cities and towns up and down the coast was a good way to explore the different areas of the three prefectures that had been hit hardest by the tsunami. I asked Junko to come, thinking it would be nice to show her what I spent all my time doing.

The volunteer group was run by a Japanese American woman I'd met in Kamaishi. She lived in Tokyo but had come to help with the relief effort in the months following the earthquake; as the process of recovery moved on, she'd started the footbath organization as a way of continuing to provide support and maintain her connection to the area. She'd made trips as far north as Kamaishi and Otsuchi, as well as to Iwaki and Minami-Souma in Fukushima.

It was mostly older women who came to warm their feet and talk with the volunteers, but, as the team Junko and I were working with was cleaning up one day, Tsuneo and his mother stopped in to check on one of their elderly neighbors.

Someone had mentioned the festival and I said that my mother owned a horse ranch back in my hometown in Washington, a couple hours south of Seattle. I explained how my mother had been fascinated by horses since the first time she'd seen one when she was growing up in Ohio. She'd wanted to become a veterinarian, but, in the late 1960s, this wasn't seen as a suitable career for a woman, so she'd settled on nursing school instead. After college, she'd gone into the army, and eventually she met my father and moved out to Washington, where land was cheap and she could finally have her horses. She always kept five or so of her own animals, and, in addition to her nursing, she ran a small business boarding other people's horses at her ranch. All in all, she had a couple dozen animals in her pastures at any one time.

She'd taught me to ride, growing up, but, around the time I hit middle school, I'd gotten more interested in comic books, and then cars, and then discovered girls. Still, I loved going back to the ranch—its wide-open spaces—and I was interested to hear what the equestrian culture was like in the coastal areas of Fukushima, which had been the domain of clans of mounted warriors for centuries.

"He's just crazy for it," Katsue said, paying no attention to the way her son shook his head. "He saves up for it every year."

"You have your own horse?" I asked.

Sitting on the floor across the table, Tsuneo told me how he always rented a horse to ride in the festival. I had been to the towns just north of Okuma and seen the small pastures out there, which usually corralled a horse or two, so I was a bit surprised he hadn't had his own animal. Then again, it made sense. Where I'd grown up, most middle-class families could afford a horse if they were so inclined, but, in Japan, land was expensive, and there wasn't much open space for riding. Tsuneo and his mother were modest people, not likely to spring for boarding and grooming fees. Tsuneo said he'd first started riding in the horse club at his high school and had been going to the festival ever since.

"Usually, the horse I rent comes from Tochigi," he said. "But they're not always used to the festival, the crowds. Sometimes it can be tough."

Katsue's elderly neighbor brought over a book of about the history of the town with photographs from the years around the time of the Second World War; I flipped through it with her, looking at the black-and-white scenes of the festival. The riders' old wooden saddles and traditional samurai armor, their metal helmets emblazoned with elaborate crests—riding in the sun in one of those would be like wearing a fur hat in midsummer. Tsuneo said they still dressed the same way, and his tone suggested he didn't mind the hardship.

"Having a home is important," I said.

"I want to see my ocean again," Katsue said.

I understood her sentiment. Though it had been a decade since I'd lived in Washington, I still thought of it as my home. Over the years, I'd wandered far afield and lived in several places that had also come to claim space in my conception of home; but to know I was physically banished from the land where I'd done my growing up would be devastating. Still, I wondered if I would remain as constant in my determination to return as Katsue and Tsuneo had.

The Sakais were so kind to Junko and me, and, before we left, they gave us a folding fan decorated with scenes of the festival, along with an old horseshoe for good luck, which we wound up leaving at the entrance to the apartment we'd moved into a half year before.

Junko and I had moved to Sendai from Ohio, where she'd been living with me until I graduated from my master's program. Before she'd come to States, we'd been doing long distance, but we were both sick of it, and I think we sensed our relationship was in danger; we needed to double down or fold up and cash out. She'd acted decisively, taking a leave of absence from the travel agency owned by her aunt and coming to Columbus on a tourist visa. She moved in with me and spent her days exploring the city and doing as she pleased. She took a single English class at Columbus State Community College before deciding the course was too easy and the downtown was too dangerous, too full of strange-looking men who yelled at her when she walked by.

We'd wound up in Sendai because the organization providing my grant was able to arrange for me to work out of a research laboratory at a university in the city. After I found out I'd been awarded the grant that would allow me to go abroad, Junko had given her final notice to her aunt, and when I moved to Japan, she relocated from her hometown to Miyagi Prefecture, a couple hours north of Tokyo by bullet train. I told myself I would either propose to her or break things off before the grant ended and I had to go back to the States. I didn't like the idea of a predetermined decision point: my parents had gone through a bitter divorce and, in order to avoid ending up in similar circumstances, I'd always told myself I would live with someone for several years before ever getting married. But my relationship with Junko confounded all my timelines. Back in Columbus, we'd once gone to see an immigration attorney about extending her visa for a few weeks, and something the lawyer said had stuck with me: "The way the laws work, they tend to force decisions faster than we might like." For three years, Junko and I had been constantly flitting back and forth between one another's countries, racking up airline miles and credit card debt, maxing out our tourist visas, drawing the suspicion and ire of the immigration authorities everywhere we went. We need stability.

This decision had been on my mind the winter I met the Sakais, and I contemplated what to do all spring. In the end, I went as far as to buy an engagement ring during a trip back to the States; I carried the ring box around in my pocket for weeks, trying to think of how I'd ask the question until I realized I couldn't go through with it. It was too much pressure. I wasn't ready. One night, Junko and I had a long, difficult conversation in which I told her that at the end of summer, I planned to return to the States alone. She'd resented me for this, and I could understand her feelings well enough. In a moment, a deep, silent chill had blown into our lives.

But then reality fell through our silence like a tree crashing through the night. Junko had started working for a company in Sendai, and, like most corporate employees, she was required to take a yearly physical. When she got the results of her health check, the X-ray turned up evidence of a worrying growth. With her father's death from cancer still fresh in her mind, she was beside herself at the thought of going in for a checkup and hearing her diagnosis.

She asked me to go with her, and it was the least I could do. We bickered all the way to the appointment, fighting even about which street to take. But after we entered the dim, disinfectant-tinged air of Sendai City Hospital, we managed to set aside our troubles. We were an odd team, shuffling from one station to another; I was impatient, leaning against the counters, tapping my foot, while she slowly wrote out her name and our address on each form presented to her. We finally found ourselves on a pair of plastic seats, where I typed nervously on my computer, ostensibly working on an essay, and she listened for her name to be called with a focused calm. She was finally summoned behind a cloth curtain, where I followed her. A portly doctor in a white lab coat gave us the bad news first: there was indeed a growth. The good news was that it wasn't aggressive. "It's probably been there for years, but no one even noticed." There was no danger to her health, no pressing need for surgery. With regular monitoring, she would be fine, though she might eventually have to have the troublesome gland removed.

As soon as we were out from behind the curtain, I let out a sigh. On the way home she took my arm, and I held her back. For the moment, we were still together, though we avoided talking about what the future held. Not long after our visit to the hospital, I'd returned to Aizu-Wakamatsu as a volunteer and had interviewed the Sakais about their lives since the disaster. The Soma Noma-Oi festival was a couple weeks away by then, and I told Tsuneo I would drive down with Junko to see him in the parade.

By the time of the third festival since the disaster, Tsuneo and Katsue were making regular trips to Okuma, but they were also beginning to see the futility of these journeys.

Not long after they'd moved into the temporary housing near Kame Koen park, they'd been issued a permit, allowing their car to get past the checkpoints into the mandatory evacuation zone. They had to pass through a radiation screening checkpoint on their way in and out of the area and they couldn't spend the night, but at least they could see their hometown without having to sneak in. Around this same time, Katsue had started helping out a flower nursery in a nearby greenhouse, pruning unneeded buds and picking up leaves.

In the spring, the owner of the greenhouse had asked her to take some flowers to her hometown as a memorial, an offering to the dead, and given her two enormous buckets of flowers. She'd been scared to go out to the ocean alone, so she went to the temporary town hall, in one of the housing clusters in Aizu-Wakamatsu, thinking someone in the administration would take the flowers off her hands. But they only told her that since she was the one who'd received the flowers, she should be the one to take them. So, not long before the spring equinox, in the days just after the one-year anniversary of the disaster, she and Tsuneo had driven out to Okuma and went to the ocean. She felt haunted by an eeriness as she set the buckets in the water and watched the flowers float off.

Since this trip, they'd returned several times, but they went straight to their own apartment now. In any case, the town was dead and empty. Slowly but surely, nature was reclaiming the land. Weeds were swallowing houses, wild boar nested in untended gardens. At their own apartment, the Sakais had long since given up on cleaning the mess left by the earthquake. All their remaining things had absorbed a good deal of radiation, and it wouldn't have been a good idea to take anything back with them to the temporary housing unit. They'd been warned against staying too long themselves, lest they expose themselves more than was safe. The best they could do was pick up the mouse turds left by the vermin that were flourishing in the deserted housing block.

But returning for the festival was something entirely different, and I could see why Tsuneo enjoyed it. For a few days a year, he got to ride with his hometown friends, who'd been scattered all over the prefecture.

I texted Tsuneo as Junko and I were driving down, and he told us to meet him in a parking lot just off the parade route, which served as a staging area. I navigated various detours through the small city, as many of the roads were blocked off, and parked in a patch of gravel behind a small store. We wove through the crowds and found the gated lot Tsuneo had mentioned.

He was a small man but, encased in the traditional armor, he seemed to have grown in stature. He stood next to his rented horse and held the reins, as the horse plunged its head into a plastic bucket of water.

"Want to try to get up?" he asked.

"I don't know if I should."

"Oh, come on," Junko said. "Give it a shot."

Hoping I could make my mother proud, I shrugged off my bag, went over, and got one foot in the wooden stirrup. After a couple of false starts, I pulled myself up, swung my leg over, and my butt landed hard in the saddle. With Tsuneo holding the reins, I managed to sit there unsteadily long enough for Junko to snap a picture with her phone.

Back on the ground, I asked Tsuneo if his mother was coming, but he told me she'd seen him ride plenty and she wasn't a horse person, so she didn't usually make it to the festival. I asked how they were doing in their temporary housing unit, and, in his way, he reassured me that they were fine. He was much quieter than his mother, especially on his own.

Junko and I said goodbye, bowing and wishing him well in the parade. We walked out of the parking lot and joined the crowds watching the procession. We looked for Tsuneo and his horse, but, in their armor, the riders were hard to tell apart; I kept thinking I saw him, only to realize it was a different horse. It was muggy, and teams of young people brought the men trays bearing paper cups of water and, incredibly, sake. I couldn't imagine drinking in that heat while riding a horse and wearing several sandbags' worth of armor.

Most of the steeds plodded across the asphalt, tired and sweating, but, now and again, an animal would come along that was fighting its rider or trying to rear up on its hind legs. One determined horse even managed to throw its rider and went cantering down the street—the people lining the sidewalks took a step back, parents pulling their children close. But the rider got to his feet, massaging his side and cursing under his breath as he trudged after his wayward mount. Judging by the laughter and jeers of the other riders, this was par for the course.

Junko eventually pointed out Tsuneo. His horse came stutter-stepping up the street, pulling the reins and working the bit in its mouth but not panicking or trying to throw him. I waved as Tsuneo made his way forward in half-turns, but all his attention was on his horse.

It was the second day of the festival, when riders from all over the region paraded through town, before arriving at the oval track in the middle of Minami-Souma City. Junko and I followed the procession to the main-event area. The leader of each group of riders would race up the middle of the grass infield and blow into a conch shell to announce their group's arrival before yelling out the number of riders in their group. This tradition was tied to the origins of the festival, which dated back over a thousand years, when it had started as a series of martial exercises: a way for the feudal lords to review the number and readiness of the troops they could call on.

The previous day had seen a series of races, with men in full samurai armor galloping on horseback down the dirt track that encircled the infield. That next day's events would focus on a competition, where young men dressed in white linen with matching headbands tried to catch one of a group of brawny, unbroken horses set loose in a field; the first horse caught was said to be chosen by the gods and would take a place of honor in the next year's procession.

But on the day Junko and I were in attendance, the main event was a game of mounted capture the flag. The hundreds of horses and riders taking part in the festival crowded into the infield, and fireworks were shot above them. When each rocket exploded, it sent out colored pieces of cloth that twisted in the wind as they fell toward the ground, where the swarm of horses and people jostled for position to try and catch the flags.

Across from the track, thousands of tourists sat on folding chairs or blankets spread out on the terraced steps of a hill and ate chicken skewers or shave ice from the food stalls. I handed the car keys to Junko and bought a beer and a plastic tray of fried chicken. We retreated to the top of the rise, and I slung my bag onto the grass as we searched for Tsuneo in the sea of riders. The fireworks popped overhead, and we watched the streamers blowing across the infield, the riders racing to where they anticipated the flags would land.

I enjoyed the tang of the watery beer and speared hunks of soggy chicken with a toothpick, giving one to Junko then one for myself. I knew if I stopped for a moment, I would feel myself boiling inside; I was angry at the situation I'd made for us. How had Junko and I spent a year together and wound up back in the same uncertain predicament? How was I leaving once again, not fully understanding where things stood between us? I hated the kind of limbo we were stuck in.

It amazed me how Tsuneo and his mother faced the undecidedness in their lives with so little bitterness or anger. After all, they were stuck in temporary housing far from their home because of other people's decisions, whereas I'd been done in by my own choices. When I'd asked the Sakais how they felt about TEPCO, they weren't even that angry. Sure, the utility had been incompetent—even years after the meltdowns at Fukushima Daiichi, they still didn't know where the fuel that had been in the reactors had wound up. But Katsue felt the government was just as responsible for letting TEPCO run the plant the way they had. They didn't care about politics or finding someone to hold responsible, or even about money. What had happened had happened. There was no returning to before.

All they wanted was to go home.

III. The Sad March of the Japanese Left

Ishinomaki City, Miyagi Prefecture

The police were outside the Ishinomaki Central Community Center. Eight cops waited in the midday sun, but they weren't expecting trouble. Last year's demonstration had been twice this size. It was five and a half years after the disaster, and the protests had gradually shrunk over time.

Inside the low-slung concrete building, people sat on folding chairs in a hardwood gymnasium. Most were well into their middle age and a few heads of white hair stood out in the audience.

Having come in late, I was in the back sweating furiously and jotting down notes. A year after finishing my grant and returning to the US, I'd come to Sendai to see Junko and attend a conference on the disaster. A couple days after I arrived, I saw an online announcement from Masami about the protest in Ishinomaki, just an hour away by train. I wanted to talk to Masami and was curious about the protest.

Now, he stood at the front of the gym holding a microphone. Pictures of his ranch hung behind him next to radiation maps of Namie and handmade banners that read: *Goodbye nuclear power*; *Make TEPCO pay the damages*; *Raise your voice—we don't need nuclear power*; and his slogan: *Unite to save lives or die trying*.

In his rough dialect, he talked about the future of his hometown. "This is the end for Namie Town. The children won't return. Daycares, elementary schools, middle schools, high schools—the buildings are still standing, but they're all closed! The kids can't come back, so the young people won't either. In the future, maybe one in ten will return to Namie. Out of a town of twenty-thousand, maybe two-thousand, mostly old men and women. What kind of town will that be? Will there be stores? Will there be a hospital? We don't know. Will there be places to work? Will we be able to grow rice or vegetables?"

The gymnasium wasn't air-conditioned. The doors were open to the breeze, and a woman in front of me fanned herself with a plastic fan. When Masami paused to point at one of the pictures, you could hear people shifting on the fake leather seats. The local organizers had set up tables along the back wall, where vendors sold tea and rice balls. On one table was a whitewashed kerosene can for donations and a stack of illustrated books about Masami's Ranch of Hope.

I'd first heard about Masami during the year I'd spent doing research on the survivors and nuclear refugees. In the weeks after the triple meltdowns at Fukushima Daiichi, Masami had gone to Tokyo to make his voice heard and tell the story of the plight of his ranch to the politicians, bureaucrats, and TEPCO executives. His message had fallen on deaf ears, and, when he'd returned, he expected to find most of his herd of cattle dead or dying in the barns where he'd left them. But, miraculously, the bulk of his animals had survived. Masami's boss, Jun Murata, had gone to the ranch and opened the barn gates. Though it was early in the spring, there was just enough grass growing in the pastures to keep most of them alive. Without regular feeding and care, a few animals had died, and others had escaped the fencing, causing damage to the neighboring properties. Masami, who was living as a refugee in Nihonmatsu, had begun coming back to his farm to feed the animals and round up the few that had escaped.

He and Jun began making trips out to the ranch every few days, ignoring the exclusion orders. The Ministry of Agriculture had ordered all the cattle be slaughtered, but Masami ignored the directive. Nor did he pay any mind to the mandatory evacuation orders. He did his best to avoid the police roadblocks, but, the few times he'd been caught and forced to sign prewritten apology statements that contained promises not to reenter the exclusion zone, he'd simply crossed out the pledges not to return.

Eventually, tired of driving out from Nihonmatsu, he decided to move back to the ranch full-time. Over time, volunteers and activists came to help with the work, and a couple even relocated to Namie themselves. The ranch had become a focal point of the antinuclear movement: a base from which Masami could drive out to Sendai, Fukushima, or even as far away as Osaka, and stage protests, often taking one of his cows with him and parading it in front of the local city hall or Ministry of Agriculture branch.

"After March 11, we don't have a village to go back to. We're weighed down with resentment. We have to unburden ourselves. We're not responsible for the disaster—it can only be TEPCO's responsibility. We're victims, refugees, nuclear survivors. Why must we destroy ourselves, be scattered about?"

He'd been speaking for an hour without notes in the Ishinomaki Community Center before he rounded into the thunderous part of his talk: "We all have to take responsibility. This will be the theme of the rest of my life, my struggle for the rest of my life. From now on, I'll go around in that speaker car and tell my story. I'll keep those cows. I'll keep them until the end... This is my cowboy. My resistance."

The day before, Masami had returned to his ranch from a protest in Hibiya Park in Tokyo. He'd slept and then driven up to Miyagi Prefecture that morning. In all, he'd been on the road for fourteen hours over the past two days. Among the jumble of maps and empty water bottles on the dashboard of his van, he kept an electric shaver that, in idle moments, he would reach for and push across his cheeks.

Though Ishinomaki had been pummeled by the tsunami in 2011, Masami was there because of the nuclear power station in the neighboring town of Onagawa. The plant had been the closest nuclear station to the quake's epicenter, but the facility had a four-story seawall as opposed to the two-story seawall at Fukushima Daiichi. Onagawa Town itself had been wiped out. One building had been ripped from the ground and pushed over by the force of the waves; its crumbling, cracked foundation lay exposed, steel rebar encrusted with hunks of concrete dangled like tree roots strung with dirt clumps. Four years later, the derelict had been left on its side in the middle of town as a monument—its fire escape zigzagged from left to right like a Penrose staircase.

"For your children, for your grandchildren, for yourselves, you have to stop the Onagawa plant. You don't need it. Shouldn't the people of Ishinomaki feel called—so strongly called—by the people of this prefecture?" For the first time, Masami's words were dissolved in applause, but he charged ahead, speaking through the cheers: "Us baby boomers have the power. The nuclear disaster was terrible, but how can we seize it, take this chance to flip the switch? I'm bursting with energy. I think I must've taken it from inside the nuclear accident. What kind of fight do the people have to put up to end the era of nuclear power? We saw it in the seventies, in the student movements, when that many people really stand up—that scene—it's different now, but isn't there a connection?"

Masami's face reddened under his farmer's tan. With his five-o'clock shadow—his hair graying around the temples, and his shirt tucked into blue jeans and cinched with a worn leather belt—he projected an air of rough masculinity; he stood ramrod straight, and his battered fingers clutched the microphone as a map of capillary veins pulsed on the back of his hand. His voice cracked, but his emotion only heightened by his coarse aspect. To watch this tough man breaking, you couldn't help but be affected. At some point his speech had lost its logical progression—from anecdote, to lesson, to call to action—and now he willed his audience to be moved.

"The disaster isn't over. We all have to stay aware of that. The 2020 Olympics are just an attempt to make us lose that awareness. Before long they'll start saying, 'Olympics, *banzai, banzai,*' and then, 'Why are those traitors quibbling with the Olympics?' Those kinds of things happen in Japan now. But we have to keep asking why in the world are we doing the Olympics? Who's getting the money? That's what we have to look for now. The bureaucrats, the politicians, the big construction companies. They're all flocking there, they'll eat the low-hanging fruit, they'll have a good time gobbling up bribes, kickbacks, rebates... But, honestly, the disaster areas aren't happy about the Olympics. In the disaster areas, all kinds of people involved in the reconstruction are packing up and going to Tokyo 'cause this... Here's what I say: 'Build a megafloat nuclear plant in Tokyo Bay.' Then people in Tokyo will get the electricity, the benefits, and the risk."

Masami wrapped up by explaining how he'd come up with a new name for his ranch—Kibo no Bokujyo, or "Ranch of Hope"—in order to turn despair into something useful, to find a new philosophy for living. The organizers thanked him, and the audience, stiff from sitting for an hour and a half, applauded and then stood. Everyone folded up their own chair and politely stacked it against one of the gymnasium's walls.

The audience filtered outside, and about half gathered at the bottom of the stairs in front of the community center, where the police stood between the crowd and the street, leaning on their red-and-white traffic batons like canes.

The event's organizers had taken the banners down from the backdrop and brought them outside, where members of the crowd held the posters in teams of two or three. A few people donned sandwich boards with antinuclear slogans, or unfolded sheets of paper printed with characters in black ink that read: *We won't allow the Abe government!* One man had a laminated sign with a cat's face that read: *Why war, meow?* A man with a gray ponytail, and an ankle bracelet above his sandals, tapped out a beat on a *djembe* drum that hung from a strap around his neck, while the protestors took up chants, alternating sayings as a kind of warm-up.

The main subject of the protest was the country's dependence on nuclear power plants. In the election the year following the tsunami in Fukushima, the Democratic Party of Japan's government had been blamed for mismanaging the response to the disaster, and the conservative Liberal Democratic Party, or LDP had taken power. The DPJ had been skeptical of nuclear energy after the triple meltdowns at Fukushima Daiichi, but, as prime minister, Shinzo Abe had called for the country's plants to be restarted, and the first reactor was scheduled to resume operations in a month. Many of the protestors in Ishinomaki feared that the Onagawa Nuclear Power Plant would be fired up soon.

Masami climbed into the passenger side of his van, with a local organizer behind the wheel, and they pulled out behind a police car, leading the march into the street. The siding around the loudspeakers mounted on the roof was painted with several of Masami's slogans, and both sides of the vehicle were plastered with stickers encouraging people to: *Search Ranch of Hope.* Hitched behind the van was a two-wheeled cart that carried a wire sculpture of a bull that had been given to him by an art professor at Kyushu University.

The drumming and chanting and Masami's voice echoing over the loudspeakers preceded the protest, and the police car's spinning lights led the march as it crawled through Ishinomaki. It was a Saturday, and people on the sidewalks in front of the stores turned to watch the spectacle: one man played an acoustic guitar as he walked among the protestors, and a woman shook a noisemaker; a second loudspeaker van brought up the rear, its sides painted with humanlike figures with wings for arms and the words *No nukes* spelled out in vines and flowers.

I jogged alongside the marchers, parallel to a journalist across the street who had a camera with a telescopic lens, which made me think twice about the pictures I'd taken with my cell phone. I'd first met Masami when I drove down to his ranch in the exclusion zone to volunteer. Junko hadn't wanted me to go and made me promise I'd throw away the work boots I'd taken with me as soon as I got home; once I returned, I found she'd bought a dosimeter, and when she passed it over the tires of the car, the needle jumped. The boots she put in several layers of plastic bags and disposed of I don't know where.

Still, it had been interesting to see Masami's ranch. Parked out front was a bulldozer with the bucket lowered to the ground; leaning against it was a sheet of spray-painted plywood that served as a warning sign: *careful of cows.* There was a whole host of other flags and signs at the entry with messages: *TEPCO and the government caused great damage!* or *Stop starving and culling animals*, as well as a couple of sun-bleached cow skulls. Inside the farm, any attempts at order had been, for the most part, discarded: the driveway was secured with a makeshift electric gate, which was just a single electrified wire stretched across the road with a hook on the end so it could be attached to a post. Masami let the cows roam the property freely, now that it was essentially worthless. Equipment lay abandoned where it had broken down or run out of fuel.

The long-term volunteers busying themselves with the afternoon feeding were generally one of two types: animal lovers or antinuclear activists. As I worked with them, shoveling hay into the feeding troughs in the two main barns, it occurred to me that these people were only the latest incarnation of the antinuclear grassroots movements that had existed from the start of the country's history with nuclear power.

Nuclear energy had arrived in the post-World War II era, as Hiroshima and Nagasaki were still being rebuilt, and even as a fishing trawler named The Lucky Dragon steamed into Tokyo Bay in 1956, having passed through the plume of a U.S. Bravo hydrogen bomb test on the Bikini Atoll, exposing the crew and its catch to radioactive fallout—though this wasn't discovered until the fish had already been sold at market—causing widespread panic. After the Second World War, with the nation's coal resources depleted from decades of strife, Japanese leaders were eager to be part of Atoms for Peace, an Eisenhower-era program to promote Cold War alliances and emphasize the civilian uses of nuclear technology. Under the initiative, America would share nuclear know-how, train foreign technicians, and even loan out fissionable materials. In the mid-1950s, the Japanese government and the country's electric utilities launched a public relations campaign about the benefits of atomic technology to reassure its nuclear-wary citizenry; one of the last vestiges of the promotion was a sign above a road in Futuba town that led to the Fukushima plant and read: *Nuclear power is the energy of a bright tomorrow.*

While antinuclear movements could cut across the political spectrum, they most often found their locus on the Left. In 1955, twenty-million signatures had been gathered for an antinuclear-weapons petition, and, in 1965, one-thousand fishing boats were mustered to protest a nuclear-recycling facility in Tokaimura.

The conservative Liberal Democratic Party of Japan, which had dominated Japanese politics since the war and tried to put down the student protests in the sixties and seventies, had also been the main driver of pro-nuclear policies. It was the party of big business, and what the conservatives often saw as the fast track to development, the liberals saw as collusion, a view that seemed borne out by the TEPCO's unresponsiveness during the disaster.

Indeed, if public opinion was to be trusted, four years after the triple meltdowns at Fukushima Daiichi, most Japanese wanted the country's existing plants to continue to operate, even if they didn't want to see the country's reliance on atomic energy increase. Immediately after the disaster, antinuclear sentiment had prevailed, and Prime Minister Naoto Kan proposed a policy similar to the German plan to focus on renewables and move away from nuclear power. But Kan's center-left Democratic Party had been swept from office, and, only two weeks after the protest in Ishinomaki, Prime Minister Abe would release a draft energy plan that saw nuclear power as a "baseload power source." Meanwhile, many experts continued to argue that the country was too prone to natural disasters to host a fleet of nuclear reactors and that the corporations and utilities that controlled the atomic power industry were too corrupt to be allowed to continue to operate.

I had seen rows upon rows of temporary housing units, where over a hundred thousand people from the areas around the nuclear plant had been relocated; these patterns of dislocation could be found in cities and towns across Fukushima Prefecture. No one had died in the meltdowns, but forty patients at the Futaba Hospital had perished in the panicked evacuation that followed. This was to say nothing of the thousands, including hundreds of young children, who'd been exposed to radioactive elements that could put them at risk for chronic diseases.

In the short term, it might make sense to run the nuclear plants, which could pass rigorous safety checks, but in the long term solar, wind, and other renewable energies were clearly safer and likely to become less expensive. This inability to imagine a future where the country wasn't reliant on electricity generated in the plants was evidence of just how captive the Japanese business and political establishment was to the nuclear industry.

The first leg of the march had wound through the districts next to the Kitakami River—abandoned buildings, empty lots, and the skeletons of new houses marking the tsunami's impact—but, before long, the route led into Ishinomaki's center and passed in front of the city hall, a three-story pink building that had once been a shopping mall. The police officers on foot hurried ahead, stopping traffic with their batons and motioning pedestrians across the blocked intersections. People lined the streets, watching as the noisy procession turned toward the train station.

But as the march left the shopping district, the spectators melted away. I trudged up a hill behind the protestors, who fanned themselves and wiped the sweat from their brows with handkerchiefs. We'd entered a residential district, and their chants echoed between quiet houses: "We don't need nuclear power! *Genpatsu* is like a house with no toilet... Leave the wealth of nature. Leave it for our children! Leave it for our grandchildren!"

I admired the marchers, their willingness to voice opposition in a society where "social harmony" is often the watchword for stifling conformity, their dedication to demonstrating during a year when they knew the crowd would be small, when the nuclear issue didn't seem as pressing as it had been four years earlier. The tsunami and Fukushima disaster had stunned the nation, but time hadn't stopped—China was getting aggressive in asserting its territorial claims in the seas to the south, America was demanding Japan play a bigger role in its own defense, and the country continued to be hampered by glacial economic growth, a shrinking population, and a national debt swollen to massive proportions.

Sure enough, when I looked closely at the marchers' signs, I noticed an array of agendas. Nuclear power was at the top of the list, but there were also people demonstrating against Japan's increasing militarization, the relocation of American military bases in Okinawa, and the new state secrecy laws, which many saw as a crackdown on press' freedoms.

This was a microcosm of politics on the national level, in which the center-left Democratic Party had fallen into disarray. Infighting among party leaders, especially party bosses Ichiro Ozawa and former Prime Minister Hatoyama, revealed new seams in the Left. Before they'd been in power, Japan's liberals were able to paper over their differences, but, as the leftist parties had joined forces, they also watered down their agenda. Once they'd won power, unable to prioritize or enact policy, internecine conflicts flared up.

After losing the majority in 2012, the party failed to garner even a quarter of the vote in the 2014 general election. Then in 2016, having steadily lost seats to the center-right and a new conservative party led by Tokyo Governor Yuriko Koike, the Democratic Party dissolved entirely. The Japanese left once splintered into factions, including the Communist Party, the Constitutional Democratic Party, and the Democratic Party for the People. With the opposition divided, the LDP had a free hand to push through a series of neoliberal reforms, despite the Abe administration's relative unpopularity.

In Ishinomaki, the protesters knew the wind was against them. You could see the resignation on their faces as they marched the last few meters of the route, ending up in front of the city's Labor Hall. Masami parked in a lot across the street and walked over to join the crowd. He stood with his hands clasped behind his back as the organizers thanked everyone for coming and announced a few upcoming events.

When the crowd began to disperse, and Masami came back toward his van, I buttonholed him, asking if he had time to talk. I still couldn't tell if he recognized me from when we'd met on his ranch, but he grunted and nodded toward his Honda. I piled in the back and one of the organizers got in the passenger seat, directing us to a hotel where the locals had gotten Masami a room. A few minutes later, I was sitting down with him in the lobby of the Ishinomaki Grand Hotel, hoping to interview him about the state of the antinuclear movement.

I couldn't help but like him. He could be difficult, gruff, and, at times, he barely seemed to register other people. And yet, there was a blunt honesty about him, a coherence to the way he moved through the world; he didn't notice people until they came within a certain physical distance, but then he treated everyone with the same earnest attention, just a notch above what he gave his animals. He had little use for pretense or formality. You knew what you were getting with him.

Before we started, I asked if he would able to talk for half an hour or so.

"Yeah," he grunted. "I'm fine here."

But I got the impression that in his mind, in the deepest part of him, he was still out there, still marching.

IV. Coffee, Hotels, & Newspapers

Otsuchi Town, Iwate Prefecture
I got off the city bus at the stop by the convenience store. It had been two and a half years since I'd been back. Everything looked different.

The last of the ruined buildings had been torn down. The debris had been picked up, sorted, and hauled away, leaving the coastal plain bare, occasional patches of weeds sprouting from the hardpacked earth. Walking toward where Kenichi Michimata's hotel and Jun Akazaki's building had once stood, I saw how the land had been built up. The reconstruction plan in Otsuchi called for raising the height of the ground in the central districts by hauling in load after load of earth in dump trucks and then using bulldozers and earthmovers to pack it into raised platforms. Homes and retail businesses would be rebuilt on these elevated areas and the rest of the town would be given over to industry—concrete mixing, cold storage, fish processing. Three years after the disaster, though they had both been structurally sound, Jun's building and the hotel, where the Caritas Otsuchi Base had operated for over two years, were both demolished.

A few months later, Jun had reopened his café in a prefab structure a short walk away from where his old building had stood, and the Caritas base had moved to another part of town. It took Kenichi longer, but he also reopened his hotel. Six Catholic priests came from all over the country to perform a Mass on the roof of the new building, where Kenichi had mounted a white statue of the Virgin Mary facing the sea. The new Kotobuki Hotel officially opened for business in October 2015.

Now, almost a year and a half after the opening, I'd come to stay at the hotel. As I walked along the road, the new city hall building came into view, enormous and white, like a block of ice sitting at the foot of the hills that lead up to the peak of Mount Shiroyama. Farther along, frames for new houses were going up on the raised land.

I heard shouts coming from one building site—a construction worker ran out of the half-finished house, threw a rock, and it clattered to the ground halfway between us. Only then, in the shadowy field below, did I see two shapes bounding at me. The deer stopped at the edge of the road. They were big and sleek and beautiful, a shimmering light-brown color. One of the deer had a rack of antlers, a massive wooden crown that magnified even the slightest turn of its head. The construction worker shouted again, and the animals flinched but didn't move.

"Get," I said under my breath, waving them across the road.

They were magnificent but could also be dangerous if they felt threatened, especially a buck trying to protect a doe. They eyed me a moment longer, then leapt across the road and into an empty plot, looking for groundcover to graze on.

I turned to the construction worker. He was a ways away, so I raised my hand to him.

"They surprised me," I yelled.

He stood there a second, saying nothing, then turned and went back inside the frame of the unfinished house. His coldness seemed out of place. When I'd worked at the hotel in Otsuchi after the disaster, there had been a camaraderie among the volunteers, even those you met for only a moment. Everyone was working together and the bonds that formed between people weren't simply friendships—though those were common enough—but a deep sense of community. After two weeks, I'd known a dozen people from the town and everyone working in the area around me.

Back then, with most of the physical and social infrastructure stripped away, social relations in the disaster area seemed to revert to a basic level. There was nothing to buy, and the jobs were replaced with the more meaningful, more necessary work of rebuilding one's life; people weren't confined to roles as customers and shopkeepers, bosses and workers. The tsunami had left a feeling of possibility in its wake, a sense that, as horrible as the disaster had been, we might yet salvage a kinder, more equitable series of relations from the waves. However, as the reconstruction effort ground on, grassroots initiatives were gradually replaced with government plans, and volunteers gave way to construction company contractors; the sense of openness and commonality gradually evaporated, and the normal divisions of society reasserted themselves.

Later on, I would meet a handful of Vietnamese men, who'd been hired as laborers by a building firm, which was putting up a tract of homes in the area. They spoke a little Japanese, but I talked to one man in English, and he told me he found the town cold, the food strange; for their part, people in Otsuchi saw the men as outsiders, and there seemed to be little fellow feeling between the laborers and the people whose houses they were building. However, through their work, at least some kind of future was coming into view for Otsuchi.

Likewise, after several years of false starts, I could finally see my own prospects a little more clearly. After my grant in Japan ended, I'd returned to the US to continue on in graduate school, while Junko stayed in Sendai. She couldn't come to the States without a visa; I'd thought about asking her to marry me, which would allow her to come as my spouse, and gone so far as to buy the engagement ring. But my doubts had overwhelmed me. I wasn't ready. I thought this would mean the end of our relationship, though we agreed to keep in touch. Still, I was surprised how she continued calling me every night. And every night I continued to pick up, giving myself a new excuse to talk to her: I was doing it for her, or this was just until I made friends in Milwaukee, where the doctoral program I'd enrolled in was. Truth was, Wisconsin wasn't a bad place, but it wasn't my place, and, without the sound of her voice, my existence there felt as thin as early-December lake ice. In the mornings, as I showered before heading to campus, I went over the reasons why I wasn't ready to throw my lot in with hers: she was a decade older than me, and I wanted to try to have children, she was as stubborn as I was, which had caused more than one blowup between us, and, like me, her emotions could be a roller coaster, and I'd always gravitated toward people who could help me maintain a more even keel. But every morning, I also felt my sense of loneliness growing.

A year after I left, I came back to Japan for an academic conference focused on the disaster and managed to be there for Masami's protest in Ishinomaki. And yet, this trip failed to resolve anything between Junko and me. I was interminably weighing the pros and cons of our relationship, but it was an equation without a solution. Now, I can see how callow I was to leave her behind like that, to not be willing to tie myself to her. Everything I'd ever asked of her, she'd done—quitting her job, moving away from her hometown, waiting for my indecisiveness to melt away.

Oh, but eventually I saw how stupid I was being. Love, I realized, isn't like filing taxes or qualifying for a mortgage. It isn't the result of ticking off a series of boxes. Like most people, I was so used to putting my decisions through a sequence of hyperrational evaluations, as if I could live my life by an algorithm: what food to eat, which road to take, what career to pursue, and even who to marry. But, for me, love wasn't a matter finding someone who met a certain number of arbitrary criteria. My relationship with Junko was more haphazard and complex than anything I could have anticipated. So much the better.

Finally, a year and a half after I'd moved back to the States, I came to my senses. I took a week off from my doctoral program, flew to Tokyo, and got a bus to Sendai. I changed into a suit in a train station bathroom and went to her office to surprise her. I proposed to her in the emergency stairwell of her building. When I'd still been lost in my idiotic, self-inflicted confusion and getting ready to depart Sendai, I'd left the engagement ring I'd bought her in our apartment. Now, when I finally was ready, I didn't have the ring on me as I got on one knee and asked if she'd marry me. In spite of all that, she said yes.

Six months later, she got a transfer to the Tokyo branch of her company, where I'd have a better chance at finding a job, and I finished my graduate coursework and immigrated to Japan to write my dissertation and look for work. We moved into a two-bedroom apartment together, and, in 2017, just a month before I came to Otsuchi, we were married by a public official in the local city office. Life with Junko suited me perfectly. I had never been particularly good at being single: the nebulous conversations with strangers in bars, the fleeting eye contact, the rhythmic pounding of one awful club after another. She and I could enjoy ourselves without leaving the house—making coffee and reading together on the sofa—and, when we did go out together, we were usually too wrapped up in our own conversations to pay much attention to anyone else. Even household chores—making the bed, hanging the laundry, cooking pasta for dinner—took on new meaning. I now had someone to witness my life.

I decided to make to a trip to Otsuchi in the last weeks before I was to begin teaching as a part-time lecturer in English at an art university in western Tokyo. I'd called and booked a room at the new Kotobuki Hotel, telling the receptionist on the phone that I was a friend of Kenichi's and would like to see him if he had time. A couple days later, he called me back, and I told him about my move to Japan. He sounded glad to hear from me and said I shouldn't worry about paying for the room. I tried to refuse him, but it was no use.

After walking past the half-built houses, I came to Otsuchi's old city hall, where the former mayor and several dozen civil servants had drowned. The derelict building was the only structure that had been struck by the tsunami and was still standing. The windows had been busted out, and the clock still pointed to 3:25 p.m., the moment when time had stopped for so many people in Otsuchi.

Behind this ruin lay the new Kotobuki Hotel: a white three-story building with solar panels on the roof and a vehicle charging station out front for the electric car Kenichi had bought. Inside, I checked in with the receptionist, who told me Kenichi would meet me after dinner.

The Michimatas were one of the most established families in Otsuchi. In addition to the hotel and newspaper distributorship that Kenichi's family owned, his cousin was a doctor with a large internal medicine practice in town. Though Kenichi had spent most of his life in Morioka, part of the reason he'd returned after the tsunami was to preserve his family's legacy.

Although Kenichi hadn't lost his home or his family, this didn't mean he hadn't suffered in his effort to revive the businesses he'd inherited, which many people might've written off as unsustainable. With one in ten of the town's residents either dead or missing, and many of those who'd survived in temporary housing, the newspaper distributorship's subscriber base had been cut in half. After his brother got divorced and moved away, Kenichi bought the business, and, in order to get it out of the red, he'd started going to sleep at six-thirty in the evening and waking up at half past two in the morning, when the early editions had to be prepared. He was still new to the town, and the delivery drivers and office workers had a hard time thinking of him as the boss. In the first year, half of his employees quit, and he'd struggled to hire new people. Still, the Michimata Distributorship was the only periodical delivery service in Otsuchi, and, within a couple years, he managed to get it back in the black and operating sustainably again.

But even as Kenichi was reviving the family concerns, his wife had stayed in Morioka, only occasionally coming to visit. I could understand why: a year after I'd first worked with Kenichi, I visited his home in Morioka and met his youngest son, Hikaru, who was on the autism spectrum. Though Kenichi's son was an adult, he'd never be able to live independently, and Kenichi and his wife had decided to care for him at home. When Kenichi moved back to Otsuchi, the town had still been without many basic services; he couldn't very well ask his family to live in the no-frills apartment he'd rented. So he lived alone, waking up well before dawn every morning and working long days while also making plans to rebuild the hotel, knowing once it was finished, it would provide a place to stay for the laborers who were needed to rebuild the town.

You could fault Kenichi for his willful nature, but there was no denying he'd helped Otsuchi move forward. And, walking out of the hotel, that was what I saw: a community taking its first steps forward after years of stasis.

I wandered over to where the former hotel had been. The last time I was there, I'd seen the mural on the side of the building that a Taiwanese artist had painted with the help of local children. Now, all the buildings were gone. What had been the center of the city, then the middle of the ruins, was a blank slate.

Before coming to Otsuchi, I'd read a newspaper article about the Buddhist cemetery in the hills near the old hotel. When I noticed a sign for Koganji Temple on the outside of a temporary structure across the street, I walked over, hoping to talk to the priest, Ryokan Ogayu, who'd been tumbled around in the waves and dug out by Jun and the other survivors in the hours after the tsunami. I wanted to ask him about the details of the aftermath.

A high voice answered my knock, and a middle-aged woman opened the door. I took her to be Ryokan's wife, who'd also been mentioned in the article, and when I said I was looking for the temple priest, she invited me inside. Her husband was sitting on the floor of the living room, relaxing in a pair of linen pajamas. He was a stocky, bald man, his head shaved so close it shone under the light. He squinted at me through his glasses.

I apologized for my intrusion, explaining that I was looking into how the disaster had affected Otsuchi and wanted to ask him a few questions. "I'm writing about Akazaki-*san*."

When I said this, he sat up. "Jun?"

"He's a friend of mine," I said.

"Why don't we go see him then?" He got up, pulling a coat over his shoulders.

I was glad for the excuse to drop in on Jun. We got into Ryokan's boxy little van, and, still in his pajamas, he drove us over to the collection of prefab structures where Jun's café and a handful of other local businesses had been set up.

The last two times I'd been there, he'd been hosting live shows featuring local bands and musicians. At these events, Jun sold beer and *shochu* cocktails instead of coffee and usually played a set with his band, Mumins. The last time, I'd watched a man with only a few gray hairs on his head dance with a woman dressed like a yoga instructor as a guy played a *djembe* drum behind them, then I'd teared up when a singer-songwriter from a neighboring community played a ballad to his hometown. But the highlight of the night was a rock band, in which all the members were dressed in mechanics' jumpsuits—it seemed they'd come straight from work.

Two years later though, when Ryokan and I arrived at Jun's shop, it was late afternoon and the quiet of the café prevailed. Jun made us coffee and then brought his pack of Mild Sevens over the table where we'd sat down. As they talked about the hours that had followed the tsunami, I listened and took notes, now and then interjecting questions about how the town had been before. After an hour, I realized I hadn't eaten and was still supposed to meet with Kenichi later. When I said I planned to get dinner at the nearby shopping center, Ryokan offered to give me a lift, saying he'd join me.

We got back in his car, and he drove us through the near-dark toward the cluster of stores, bars, and restaurants, which had opened in three temporary two-story structures that had been erected on the soccer field of an elementary school.

I had also been to the shopping center before. When Kenichi had asked me to help him hand out food to the survivors. This had been right after the block of stores had been built, the winter following the disaster, and the U-shape made by the buildings was bustling with people. Kenichi was always one for grand gestures, and this had been a way to reintroduce himself to the town and promote the newly opened Caritas base camp at the hotel.

He'd stood there, in the middle of the parking lot, shouting: "Rations, emergency rations! Please come eat!"

I was next to him in the cold, handing out sweet, skewered dumplings, which we'd charred on a gas burner. It took only a couple hours to run out of food, but Kenichi looked happy by the end of it. I think he liked feeling he was doing something for the people.

When Ryokan and I arrived at the shopping center, it was Sunday night, and only a few places were still open. He parked and led me upstairs to a seafood restaurant. I'd talked with Buddhist priests before, but it was interesting to hear about life as a spiritual figure in a port town. His family had been part of the community for generations, and they'd adapted to life there; Ryokan didn't follow the Buddhist injunctions against eating fish, as his parishioners were constantly bringing him the prize of their catch. They wouldn't understand if he refused their offerings. For this same reason, he didn't turn down the bottles of sake they gifted him either.

When I mentioned I was a friend of Kenichi and was meeting up with him later on, Ryokan asked if I belonged to a church and I shook my head. I'd never found the faith I'd searched for after my grandfather's death, when I was working as a volunteer. I'd been learning more about Buddhism, but I was far from a believer.

"Do you believe in God?" he asked, and I took this to mean the Christian idea of the Lord.

Through all my searching, the only conclusion I'd come to was that, for me, belief was bound up with people. I'd always felt empathy with those around me—I found people, even total strangers, fascinating and full of spontaneous grace. Of course, these moments of openness were just as often buried by mundane concerns or covered by a layer of cynicism, but this sensibility was also what had led me to writing. In prose, I found an excuse to pay very close attention to humanity.

I told Ryokan I didn't know about God, but I felt there was a kind of connection between all living things.

"Good, good," he said. "This's important."

In spite of what Ryokan's said, I knew it sounded like drivel. Still, it was the best I'd come up with. The idea of an affinity shared between all life lay at the center of so many of my values. If nothing else, one function of living things was to ascribe meaning to an otherwise cold, dead universe. In a way, writing, as I understood it, was also the act of discovering meaning within chaos, of finding a narrative signal inside the confusion of the world.

After we finished dinner, including a couple carafes of sake, Ryokan called for a car service that sent a vehicle for us with an extra driver who got behind the wheel of Ryokan's little van while we rode in the backseat of the following car. Kenichi had told me to come to his house, and I gave his address to the driver. When the car service dropped me off, Kenichi was waiting out front, in the midwinter dark. The two cars drove away, and he led me inside. On a shelf beside the entryway was a striking, brightly colored picture of Mary, her head encircled in a golden halo.

I took off my shoes, and Kenichi took me on a tour of his house, which the builders had finished only a few months before. For the most part, the rooms were bare, sparsely furnished; the house seemed empty, unlived in almost. In his room, there was a single lonely futon spread out on the floor, a ball of mussed sheets and blankets on top of it.

Kenichi led us in a circle around the first floor, until we'd returned to the kitchen and dining room near the front.

He brought out two cardboard boxes. "What will you drink? Red or white?"

One thing I'd always liked about Kenichi was how straightforward he was. To him, wine was wine, and he had no time for any nonsense about vintage or viniculture. He seemed to approach religion the same way—once he'd accepted Jesus, the rest followed: the virgin birth, the miracles, the resurrection. The Lord had ascended to heaven, where he lived with our Father, and would admit those who asked for forgiveness. In this orthodox light, all of my vacillations about faith seemed so inconsequential. Kenichi's framework lacked the fine distinctions I spent so much time making, but I had to admit, in many ways, it was simpler, more powerful.

As usual, I gave myself over to his influence: "Let's have red then."

He poured me a stout drink, and I returned the favor, giving him a tall glass. I told him about my life since I'd last seen him: marrying Junko, moving to Japan and finding my first job. Having never been one for pictures, the only photo I had to show him was of Junko and me at the French bistro where we'd gone after getting married at the local ward office. We were sitting at the table, grinning awkwardly, both of us holding one side of our marriage certificate.

I asked about him, and he told me how hard it had been to get the newspaper distributorship on steady ground while also overseeing the last of the construction on the hotel. He was glad he'd completed it when he had; he was worried the rooms would soon be empty because another, larger hotel was going up nearby. The work had taken a toll, and he said he'd lost weight from the stress. He was indeed skinnier, especially around the face. His hair had gone from salt-and-pepper to a whitish gray.

"I had troubles," he said. "But now my eldest son is here. He's the boss now."

"What about you?" I said. "What are you going to do?"

"Me?" He seemed surprised to be asked. By this point, we were both on our third or fourth glass. "I'm going to travel. Go to Italy. See the Vatican. Go to Europe with my wife and see Notre Dame, all the great cathedrals." He said he wanted to hike the Way of Saint James, walking the sacred route to the shrine of the apostle in northern Spain.

"Well, I'm glad to see you're happy."

I reached over to pour myself another, but we'd drank the last of the red. We had a good laugh at this and then moved on to the other box. After a couple glasses of the metallic "California White," Kenichi was looking sleepy and my sense of time was blurring. I knew I should get out of there if I was going to have any chance of waking up in time for checkout the next day.

Kenichi called me a taxi, and I took it back to the hotel, where I fumbled with my shoes in the front entrance before stumbling up to my room.

February 20

I woke feeling surprisingly well and had breakfast in the hotel's dining room downstairs. One of the difficulties Kenichi had faced was finding a cook for the hotel. The first person he'd hired hadn't known how to run such a large kitchen and eventually quit. Kenichi resorted to buying frozen meals and reheating them, but this wasn't a real solution. By the time I arrived, he'd hired a few local women to run the kitchen, and the breakfast of seared salmon, rice, and miso soup was delicious.

After I'd eaten, I checked out, leaving my bag at the reception desk, and went over to Jun's place. He quietly smoked as he made me a cup of coffee, and I looked over my notes from our conversation the day before. I jotted down a few follow-up questions for him and his mother, and they answered my queries as I sipped the steaming cup he'd set in front of me.

My bus back to Tokyo wasn't until the evening, so, once I was out of questions and coffee, I said goodbye to Jun and his mother and walked out of the café. I headed to MAST, an indoor mall on the edge of the tsunami-affected area, where I thought I might write until I got hungry enough for lunch. In the food court, I sat down at a table and opened my laptop. After a couple hours, I thought to take a break and call Junko, figuring she might've stepped out for lunch by then. The cavernous interior of the mall was hushed in the hours before noon, so I got out my phone and went to stand between the two automatic doors at the front entrance. I saw Kenichi crossing the parking lot toward me.

"What are you doing here?" he asked, as I slid my phone back in my pocket.

"I was about to call my wife and then get lunch."

"We drank up all my wine, so I came to buy more," he said. "Well, let's eat."

I gathered up my laptop and followed Kenichi back out into the parking lot. He drove us to a restaurant on the other side of town and asked me a little about Junko as we ate, though, for the most part, we were both quiet.

Now, I wish I'd talked with Kenichi more about his family, his boys, who he'd asked to move to Otsuchi to help him. Maybe then he would've told me about his middle son. A couple years before, Kenichi had mentioned that his son Kei had become a shut-in after moving into the apartment in Otsuchi, but on the day we had lunch, I didn't know that Kei had taken his own life several months before. Maybe if I'd given Kenichi a chance to tell me, some measure of the weight would've lifted off him. Then again, even if I'd asked, maybe Kenichi wouldn't have said anything.

But I was too blind to think to ask him about these things. No, when I'd seen Kenichi crossing the parking lot toward the mall, I'd seen my happy old friend. I'd seen a man who'd nearly worn himself out with work but was now enjoying his retirement, drinking wine late into the night. I saw the straightforward man I'd convinced myself to see.

What I didn't see was a man who'd lost his stepmother in the disaster, and then become estranged from his brother. I didn't see a man who'd asked his sons to come help him reestablish his family in Otsuchi, only for one of his boys to commit suicide after he moved into the house Kenichi had built. I didn't see the complicated, difficult side of Kenichi's life because I didn't let myself.

In fact, it was the last meal I would ever share with Kenichi. I returned to Otsuchi in the summer and stayed at the Kotobuki Hotel again, but the receptionist told me he was out of town, in Morioka. I hoped he was with his wife and his family, but I would later learn he'd spent his last months in a hospital there.

Less than a year later, a mutual friend told me Kenichi had died just a few days after the seventh anniversary of the disaster. She showed me the photo of his face before he was cremated, his eyes closed. It was horrible. He'd lost so much weight. His skin was all shriveled, he was almost unrecognizable. Almost, but not quite. I still recognized my old friend; he was there, warped by all he'd experienced since I'd met him.

I asked around, but no one ever gave me a straight answer as to what Kenichi had died from. Everyone I talked to simply said he'd been through so much stress, like saying he'd died of a broken heart. There was also a rumor he'd had a rare brain condition. I only hope he didn't suffer so much. He was sixty-three years old, and I still miss him.

But that isn't how I want to remember Kenichi. I want to remember him the way he was when we were working together, when we'd take a break and he would tell me about his plans for the new hotel he was going to build—how many floors there would be and the different kinds of rooms it would have. I want to remember the way a smile would pull over his face as, even in the midst of our labor, he was making plans and thinking of the next job, filled with excitement as he looked toward a better future—a brighter one. Already, he could see what came next.

Epilogue

September 2018

I. Forgetting

Like so many of the government's policies—Abenomics or the recent immigration reforms—reconstruction in the areas most directly affected by the tsunami has been a mix of incremental successes, missed opportunities, and complete failures of imagination. As terrible as it was to watch the ocean rise up and reach inland like a massive claw, ripping out homes, families, and entire villages, it also forced those who were left to try and start their lives anew. For decades before the tsunami, the towns and cities of coastal Iwate, Miyagi, and Fukushima Prefecture had been deindustrializing, depopulating, and generally declining. Many thought 2011 could be a turning point.

Instead, national and local politicians doubled down on the strategies that had served them in the past. Often, this meant large-scale construction projects, such as the redesigned Kamaishi Recovery Memorial Stadium, or the network of new highways in Fukushima, or the rebuilt seawalls in Ryoishi and the land-raising projects in cities and towns up and down the coast. Even the 2020 Olympics—which, despite the fact that many of the stadiums are still under construction and a single athlete has yet to take a single field, are estimated to cost twice as much as when they were proposed—are a rerun of Tokyo's hosting of the Games in 1964.

In most cases, these plans have provided communities with jobs and a temporary infusion of cash, while also serving the interests of big business and construction conglomerates. In Kamaishi, an Aeon Town Mall was built and promptly filled with national chain stores, like Uniqlo and Daiso. A few blocks away, two new pachinko slot-machine parlors have gone up, and their parking lots are almost continually filled. Lawson and 7-11 convenience stores have reappeared in Otsuchi, selling cigarettes and box lunches to the crews of construction workers who've come to build a new post office, library, and community center for the town.

After the devastation, new infrastructure was certainly needed, and these projects have helped pull disaster-affected communities back from the cliff's edge they faced in the days after the tsunami. But look a little further down the road, past the warning signs of population decline, urbanization, industrial concentration in and around Tokyo, and the future of Tohoku falls into darkness. Indeed, in Kamaishi and Otsuchi, local businesses have struggled to get back on their feet.

For Keitaro Matsumoto, the tsunami was a calamity he has yet to overcome. He was able to reopen his hair salon in a space within his temporary housing cluster, where he ran it for seven years. But when he moved into a newly built recovery housing block—a kind of subsidized house—he was unable to run his business out of the apartment or afford the monthly rent on a commercial property, and he had to close Hair Studio K. Instead, he signed a contract with Kamaishi's Health Care Center to do home visits, giving haircuts to the elderly, disabled, and others who can't leave their houses. Now in his sixties, Keitaro feels he still has a few working years left. He wants to reopen his salon but doesn't know if he'll be able to.

Ryoishi, the district where his family's home had been, adopted a reconstruction plan similar to the enormous earthworks project in Otsuchi. Tons of dirt are being brought in to raise the level of the ground, and the basin that the small hamlet is nestled in has been transformed. Mounds of packed earth several stories tall cover the valley floor.

North of Kamaishi, Jun Akazaki reopened his café, six and a half years after the disaster, in a building attached to his and his mother's new home. The number of structures dotting Otsuchi's raised central districts has multiplied, and, gradually, the shape of the town has come into view: the neighborhoods are smaller, more compact, and are centered around a park and a new library that contains a memorial to the tsunami. Other aspects of the Honcho and Omachi districts have also been restored; the section of Japan Rail's Yamada Line between Miyako and Kamaishi has been rebuilt and sold from JR to the Sanriku Tetsudo, a private company, which revived service on the line eight years after the tracks were washed away.

Compared to the towns and cities damaged primarily by the tsunami, the recovery in the area around Fukushima Daiichi is moving forward at a crawl. Teams of workers have spent years sweeping up topsoil and leaves in the mandatory evacuation zone, but it's unclear if their efforts have reduced radiation levels any faster than natural decay would have. What these interventions have produced is thousands of black bags of contaminated soil, which no other town or prefecture is willing to dispose of. Outside each deserted town, piles of plastic-covered sediment sit in black stacks, some as large as a soccer field.

Likewise, over the years, hundreds of temporary holding tanks assembled on the grounds of the nuclear power plant have slowly filled with radioactive wastewater, a byproduct of the process of cooling the damaged reactors. The amount of cancer-causing cesium in the water is above the level allowed for release into the environment and can be removed only through a complex filtration system. But, with over a million tons of water already stored around the TEPCO facility, and in spite of public opposition, the utility has considered dumping contaminated water into the Pacific, which would pose a further risk to Fukushima's already battered fisheries.

Meanwhile, engineers have only recently managed to use robots outfitted with cameras to look inside the damaged reactors. Decommissioning the plant itself will take decades and involve building an enormous roof over the Unit Three reactor in order to remove the fuel rods.

In all, the financial cost of the nuclear disaster is estimated be more than sixty times the price of the 2020 Olympics, to say nothing of the dozens of people—many of them patients at the nearby Futaba Hospital—who lost their lives in the evacuation. And yet, not one TEPCO executive has gone to jail or been stripped of the compensation they received from the company. Masataka Shimizu, the utility's former president who went missing at the height of the disaster, has landed on his feet: having resigned after the triple meltdowns, in the year following the disaster, he became an outside director of Fuji Oil. The company's largest shareholder is TEPCO.

Considering all this, it's understandable why Masami Yoshizawa is still angry. In the years since I saw his speech in Ishinomaki, he's continued his antinuclear power campaign, keeping TEPCO, government regulators, and the bureaucrats who enabled such projects at the core of his protests.

When the mayor of Namie Town died in 2018, Masami ran an insurgent campaign in the special election to replace him. Along with a few long-term volunteers, Masami mobilized the network of activists, which had sprung up around his farm, using his email newsletter to ask for donations and support. In his campaign, he promised to sue TEPCO for further compensation, prevent the dumping of wastewater into the ocean, and to repurpose Namie's contaminated rice fields to grow crops for ethanol, so that the ruins left behind by an old, malign energy source might become the starting point for a new alternative. Yet, this message proved too radical for voters, and Masami lost in a landslide to the chairman of the former mayor's support group.

He still lives on the Ranch of Hope in Namie, feeding his herd of irradiated cattle with donations from like-minded activists and sympathetic farmers: shipments of pineapple husks, apple dregs, and bean sprout refuse arrive in truckloads from all over the country. For as long as he lives, he has pledged to keep fighting the powers that, somehow, continue to be.

If anything, Katsue and Tsuneo Sakai are almost the mirror image of Masami. When ordered to leave their hometown, they evacuated, and, for over eight years, they've lived as nuclear refugees. On balance, they've followed the directives of local and federal officials. They don't even place much of the blame for their many misfortunes on the government or

TEPCO. In Katsue's words, "When they built the plant, it brought life to the town. No one said anything back then."

The only mandate they haven't followed is the unspoken one taken up by so many of their neighbors: forget your hometown; put away your desire to return; move on with your life. While many of the nuclear refugees have found jobs in the areas they were relocated to, or in other parts of the country, and restarted their lives, the Sakais have held fast to their desire to someday go home. It's for evacuees like them that the government continues trying to decontaminate parcels of land in seven towns around the plant, so that reconstruction efforts might at last begin. However, in Namie, one of the towns that is furthest along in this process, of the roughly eighteen thousand officially registered residents, fewer than eight hundred have returned to live in the small area where the evacuation orders have been lifted.

At first, Katsue thought she would be able to go back to Okuma after two years, but two years have come and gone four times over, and Katsue's confidence that she would someday go home has diminished. She used to say, "Once the parents move back, the children will come... They say they won't come back. But once we can live again, they'll come." However, this was before their much-loved cat, Coo, died in the temporary housing. This was before Katsue herself was diagnosed with cancer and had to have surgery to remove her ovaries.

Now, when she talks about the prospect of returning to Okuma, a hint of bitterness creeps into her voice. In an offhand remark, she says she thinks the government is just cleaning up Fukushima as a PR stunt for the Olympics. Tsuneo chimes in, saying they won't let us go back until the Games are over.

The shaking of the Great Tohoku Earthquake and Tsunami stilled almost a decade ago, yet it still reverberates through communities up and down the coast. After the waves came, everyone I met in Tohoku had been shaken, and, in a few cases, the tremors had opened up rifts in their lives. Keitaro Matsumoto lost his stability in the disaster, and, in due course, the reconstruction effort would strip him of his business and a measure of his pride. The nuclear disaster took everything from Masami Yoshizawa, save for his land, his cattle, and his radical mindset.

For others, the vibrations forced them to cling to what was most important, what remained the of the things that really matter. Jun Akazaki has rededicated himself to his friends and family, his music, and his café. Katsue and Tsuneo Sakai hold stubbornly on to their hometown, or at least to the idea of it, even as the place itself has grown remote to them, and the town has turned into a collapsing ruin, overgrown with weeds and populated by deer and wild boar.

In this way, I also stubbornly cleave to the handful of people and half-dozen places that have been important in my life. In Tohoku, I learned there may be no profit in devotion, no advantage in obstinacy, but there is power in refusal, and there is meaning in persistence. Even as the northeastern region depopulates, even as the government in Tokyo focuses more and more on its own needs, I hold fast to the knowledge that a different future is still possible.

In the months after the disaster, I saw a different version of the country. A version unlike the Tokyo of today, where crowds of commuters ignore the growing homeless population and the main function of politics seems to be managing decline. Often, the public discourse implicitly suggests that nothing can be done to solve the society's largest problems—even acknowledging the staggering issues facing Japan might be going too far. Reality stands in the way of anything that might radically move the country toward some brighter, better place.

This story, about the way things are and about how they couldn't be any other way, is a story told by people who don't want change. But there is another story. A story about how, even in the middle of the wreckage, people found hope and spun joy out of thin air.

A story with scenes like the night the coffee shop Mumins reopened in a temporary little building near where the city hall had been: a tiny point of light in the middle of the dark, ruined town. Muffled strains of music drifting out the front door, while in back Jun was serving drinks, and, in front, still in their work overalls, a rock band was playing to a few dozen well-lubricated locals. When the guitarist started his solo, launching himself into the crowd, it looked as if he was going to come unplugged—with a hiss of static, the song would cut out right at the peak. But then, a man in a leather jacket picked up the cord and handed it over his head to the person next to him, and the guitarist went deeper into the clutch of warm bodies. Hands kept jutting out of the crowd to lift the cord higher, passing it over, and the guitarist was making a circle now, everyone in the crowd chanting, "Go! Go! Go!" as people pitched in to keep the cord from catching or tangling, and one of the band members near the speakers in front straightened out the kinks until the guitarist, sweat beading on his forehead, completed his circle, returned to the front, and finished his solo, hammering away at the final cord.

There are stories like these, stories of a better world, which might emerge if only we would let it.

Acknowledgements

This book is primarily based on the lives and experiences of Keitaro Matsumoto, Jun Akazaki, Tsuneo and Katsue Sakai, and Masami Yoshizawa. Their willingness to tell their stories and share the most intimate details of their lives over the course of dozens of interviews made this project possible. Their kindness, their warmth, and their strength are emblematic of the people of Tohoku.

I also would never have had the chance to volunteer with communities affected by the disaster had it not been for the organizations that have helped to rebuild the Tohoku region. I am particularly indebted to Caritas Japan, especially the volunteers at the Haramachi Base, the Kamaishi Base, and the now-closed Otsuchi Base. In particular, I want to thank Seiko Ise, Hironori Hiramatsu, the late Father Funayama, and the late Father Furuki. I also owe a debt of gratitude to Kerry Anne O'Conner and Masayuki Kubota, of the Ashi-yu-Tai, and the incomparable artist Joe Wu, who so generously donated his time and talent to the people of Ishinomaki.

During the eight years I was at work on this manuscript, I received support and editorial guidance from more individuals and institutions than I can possibly name here. However, I would like to express my appreciation for the writers and teachers at The Ohio State University's MFA Program in Creative Writing, especially the late Lee K. Abbott, who read early chapters of this book and gave encouragement to their fledgling author. You were right about everything, Lee. My research was also supported by an Alumni Grant for Graduate Research & Scholarship from the university's graduate school. I am grateful to the Fulbright Program and the US-Japan Educational Commission, which took me on as a Graduate Research Fellow; the International Research Institute of Disaster Science (IRIDeS) at Tohoku University hosted me during the year I lived in Sendai, and Professor Akira Mano tutored me in the finer points of the geological mechanisms underlying earthquakes. In addition, my travel and presentations of my research at various conferences were supported by the University of Wisconsin-Milwaukee's English PhD Program and by my current institutional home, the Center for Education of Global Communication at the University of Tsukuba, where Kiyoe Kashiwagi has always been on hand to help. I would also like to extend my gratitude to the Japanese Studies program at Dartmouth College, with special thanks to James Dorsey, who reminded me several times to "just finish the damn book."

My understanding of disaster, recovery, and the nuclear power industry was influenced by the works of many researchers and scholars, including Rebecca Solnit's *A Paradise Built in Hell: The Extraordinary Communities That Arise in Disaster* (2009), Daniel Aldrich's *Site Fights: Divisive Facilities and Civil Society in Japan and the West* (2010) and *Building Resilience: Social Capital in Post-Disaster Recovery* (2012), Tsutomu Harigaya's *Genpatsu Ikki* (2012), Richard Samuel's *3.11: Disaster and Change in Japan* (2013) and *Fukushima: The Story of a Nuclear Disaster* (2014) by Lochbaum, Lyman, Stranahan and the Union of Concerned Scientists. In addition, there were several individuals who helped with my research, including the former New York Times Tokyo Bureau Chief, Martin Fackler, and Asian Press Front's Masakane Kinomura.

Kenichi Michimata, the late proprietor of Kotobuki Hotel in Otsuchi, gave me the aid of his friendship, and I am aggrieved every time I remember he is no longer with us. In Mutsu City, Sachiko Nakanishi, Suzuko Fujisawa, and Mariko Kawashima helped me feel I was part of their community. Michiaki Ogura, my constant writing partner in Tokyo, read, translated, and gave me feedback on this project at crucial points.

Of course, this book would not have been possible without the support of my family, especially my mother and father, Marjorie Ward and James Larson. Also, my host family in Japan, Kazuko and Koji Gokita and Akemi and Jamie Reay, who opened their home to me when I first arrived in Chiba and have welcomed me back time and again.

Finally, if I accomplished anything of value, which was not due to the efforts of those listed above, then in all likelihood it was due to the love and kindness of my wife, Junko Takagi.

—Tokyo, October 2019

About the Author

MW Larson is an author, editor, and translator based in Tokyo. He earned his MFA at The Ohio State University and is currently a doctoral candidate at the University of Wisconsin-Milwaukee. A former Fulbright scholar, he has published fiction and nonfiction in in *Colorado Review, Portland Review, Los Angeles Review of Books, Ninth Letter,* and *Witness.* He lives with his wife in Tokyo and teaches English and writing at the University of Tsukuba.

CPSIA information can be obtained
at www.ICGtesting.com
Printed in the USA
BVHW032342090320
574562BV00001B/1